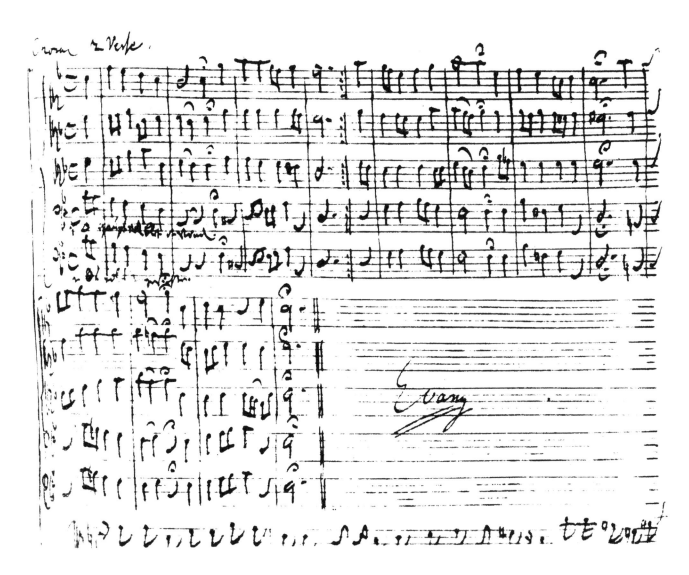

Fac-simile from Bach's manuscript of the "St. Matthew Passion" showing the chorale "Herzlich thut mich verlangen" (beginning "O Haupt voll Blut und Wunden", No. 17 in this volume)

CHORALES

By

JOHANN SEBASTIAN BACH

Selected and Edited by

CHARLES N. BOYD

A N D

ALBERT RIEMENSCHNEIDER

CHORALES 1-91

Ed. 1628

G. SCHIRMER, *Inc.*

DISTRIBUTED BY

HAL•LEONARD®
CORPORATION
7777 W. BLUEMOUND RD. P.O. BOX 13819 MILWAUKEE, WI 53213

PREFACE
THE CHORALES AS AN APPROACH TO THE APPRECIATION OF BACH

The value of Bach's music is only now beginning to be realized, two centuries after his passing. The people of his own time and the half-century immediately following his death were not ready to appreciate it; and, in fact, all things seem to have combined against their doing so. The greater part of Bach's composition is for the voice, consisting of music composed to words. The most readily understood of this music is the group known as the harmonized chorales. In this form we find stated in a simple manner the very heart and essence of Bach's creative work. During the Rationalistic Period, which reached its height after Bach's death, the chorale fell into disrepute along with other forms of church music, with the result that Bach's vocal music became more and more neglected. Only a few understanding souls kept a small interest in it alive.

The reader will note that throughout this volume each chorale is given the German title by which its tune is best known. This title is usually the first line, complete or incomplete, of the hymn with which the tune was most commonly sung. Each harmonization, however, was intended to serve, not all stanzas of the hymn in question, but only the particular one or ones Bach chose as being appropriate to the position in which he placed it, in the course of one of his cantatas, passions, or oratorios. The importance of this point, briefly developed in this discussion, will become apparent to the student as his familiarity with the chorales increases. Meanwhile, it will explain why many of the chorales bear titles which seem to have no relation to their texts: the name of the tune comes from the first stanza, while the text of any individual harmonization may be the third, or the thirteenth. For the title in English the first line of the translation of the particular stanza used has been adopted.

We know now through the aesthetic studies made by Rochlitz, Mosewius, Schering, Pirro, Schweitzer, and others, that the essence of Bach's method was to let the words influence his music, which thus has a pervadingly symbolic and descriptive character. This character is produced largely by the voice-leading. But harmonic changes of varied hues and colors, subtly matching the meanings of the text, are also continually in evidence. A careful comparative study of the different settings and keys for the various stanzas of the same chorale tune in the "St. Matthew Passion", or in the motet "Jesu, Priceless Treasure", will show clearly why a different harmonization was used for each, instead of the repetition of one already used.

It was only because the words underlying Bach's harmonizations were ignored that such a ludicrous blunder could be committed as that of Abt Vogler and Carl Maria von Weber in publishing twelve of Bach's chorale harmonizations, placing directly opposite each one an "improved version" by Vogler. Vogler also arranged a composite consisting of parts of several of Bach's harmonizations of the same tune and then proceeded to criticize it. Had the words accompanied the chorales, this would have been unthinkable, since the association of words and music would have permitted an insight into some of the conditions which Vogler called inconsistencies. A hundred years later Widor made the statement to Schweitzer that the logic of the great fugues was always apparent to him, but that certain progressions in the chorale-preludes seemed entirely irrelevant. Schweitzer replied that a knowledge of the underlying words would clear up any doubts, and it did so to the satisfaction of the great French organist.

Although the Bach chorales are the best approach to Bach, history shows that almost every step undertaken in their publication was made with an awkwardness truly incomprehensible.

The first steps in the history of the publication of Bach's chorale-settings were the editions published by Birnstiel, of 100 of these chorales, edited by Marpurg, and supplied with a preface and a list of errors by C. P. E. Bach, in 1765, and of a second 100, edited by J. F. Agricola, in 1769. These were followed in 1784-1787 by an issue of 371 published by Johann Gottlob Immanuel Breitkopf, from a manuscript of C. P. E. Bach. These 371 chorales were supposed to represent the complete list of Bach's four-part chorales. The unfortunate feature of Breitkopf's edition was that the chorales were all published without the words to which they had been composed, thus leaving the most important clue to their full comprehension entirely out of the picture. Since then, about 100 of the cantatas and larger vocal works which Bach composed are definitely known to have been lost. In the complete published compositions of Bach there are found a few more than 200 chorale harmonizations associated with the words to which they were composed. Approximately an equal number of existing Bach chorales belong to that class of which the words have been lost with the cantatas, etc. The music of these latter chorales has been preserved only through the medium of the 1784-1787 edition mentioned above.

In many chorale harmonizations the tone-painting is so definite as to form patterns and clusters of what Schweitzer calls Bach's musical language. It is to be hoped that some day a keen and intelligently directed research along these lines will attempt to restore to us the words to which these chorales were originally harmonized. One of Bach's admonitions to his students was to give special consideration to the words while accompanying the chorale in the church service.

Breitkopf's succeeding edition of the chorales, in 1832, was but a reprint in oblong format of the edition of 1784-1787. The thought of adding the words does not seem to have occurred to the publisher. This became the most widely used edition. A few years later (1843) Robert Friese of Leipzig published an edition edited by C. F. Becker in open score, in the C-clefs, in which, for some inexplicable reason, all of the harmonizations of the same chorale were given in the same key. The transposition necessary for this purpose was a very bad feature of this edition. And still no words were associated with the music.

In 1850 and 1865 the Edition Peters, under the editorship of Ludwig C. Erk, published two volumes of chorales, giving the words wherever their relationship to the music could be established. Erk did a splendid and scholarly piece of research and opened the way for a better comprehension of these important creations of the great master. Most of this was done before the Bachgesellschaft Edition began to appear, and represented a great advance over all previous publications.

In the Bachgesellschaft Edition, every chorale to which the originally associated words are known appeared in the composition of which it formed a part.

This left about 185 "orphan" chorales which found no place because the complete work in which they had originally appeared had been lost. Using the 1784-1787 edition as a basis, Dr. Franz Wuellner collected these in a separate volume for this edition, a volume which was merely a duplication of previous efforts and added nothing. Only the first stanza of each hymn was added to the tune with which that hymn was usually associated.

In 1898 Breitkopf & Härtel published an edition consisting of 389 chorales, under the editorship of B. F. Richter, in which words were placed to all of the harmonizations. For the chorales to which the words were missing, the name of the chorale-tune determined the selection of the words, without regard to the musical content, and thus what should have been arrived at by deep study and research was supplied only by conjectural methods. This again was a misleading approach to the clarification of the situation.

A splendid edition in open score and in the proper C-clefs was published by Bote & Bock under the editorship of W. Bargiel in the early nineties. The words belonging to each chorale appear in their proper places, and those harmonizations to which the words have been lost are printed without words. This excellent edition has been reported out of print for some time, and is difficult to secure. Bargiel repeated numerous errors made in former editions, especially those resulting from a condensation of the vocal bass and *Continuo* parts.

A few years ago H. Elliot Button compiled for Novello and Company, Ltd., an edition of the chorales in which, strange to say, no words were used with the music. A feature of unusual ingenuity is a melodic index by which one may easily identify any one of the Bach chorales. This seems to be the chief contribution of this edition.

Outstanding work on Bach chorales was done by the late Dr. Charles Sanford Terry. His studies, published by the Cambridge University Press in three volumes, contain much material which is the result of exhaustive research. His *J. S. Bach's Four-Part Chorals*, published by the Oxford University Press, is perhaps the best work covering this subject. The chorales appear in short score; and, in connection with each, several stanzas are presented with German and English words. Wherever the words can be identified as belonging to the music, Terry indicated with an asterisk which stanza Bach used. Terry conceived the chorale as a hymn to be sung in several stanzas by the congregation.

From the foregoing it can readily be seen that in

turning from a bare presentation of the music of the chorales without words, as in the earliest editions, to an attempt to make of them independent congregational hymns,* we are coming no closer to Bach's intentions. It must be understood that Bach specifically harmonized these chorales as parts of larger vocal works and, in the majority of cases, used only one stanza of the words for each setting. In a few exceptional cases two stanzas were used. In such cases the music is designed to fit both stanzas — but not others. Whether in the course of the presentation of the work the choir or the congregation sang the chorales, the fact remains that these compositions were part and parcel of the larger work and not conceived as independent congregational hymns. When Bach wrote or arranged chorales as hymns, as he did for Schemelli's *Gesangbuch*, he presented only the melody and a bass which was supplied with appropriate figures to indicate to the organist a basis upon which he could produce an accompaniment to agree with the words.

It should be noted, too, that *in practically every case an orchestra is associated with his chorale-harmonizations.* This is definitely in disagreement with the practice of singing these works for unaccompanied chorus.

Recognition of the importance of the Bach chorale-harmonizations is growing apace. Prominent music schools, including the Paris Conservatoire, have established courses devoted to the study of them. It is therefore appropriate that a text be provided which will offer students *an exact reproduction of Bach's work.* It will always remain true that complete study and research necessitate a comparison with the chorale in its original setting in the orchestral score, made available by the Bachgesellschaft Edition. Much may be accomplished, however, with a basic text presented in its correct form. This edition is presented as such a text.

The more one studies these master-creations, the more one is convinced that the real solution of their mystery will be found by following Bach's directions and intentions implicitly. This much accomplished, the key to a comprehensive understanding of the rest of Bach's work is made more available.

The incentive for the preparation of this edition came from a discussion at the annual meeting, in Philadelphia, of the National Association of Schools of Music in December, 1935. Modern teaching of

harmony and counterpoint is constantly making wider use of the C-clefs; but suitable material for familiarizing the student with the use of these clefs has not been easily obtainable. One incidental purpose of this edition is to supply that need. But merely to reprint a group of chorales in score would ignore the great possibilities inherent in these extraordinary works of Bach. Here, not only is the opportunity provided for acquiring a more fluent use of the clefs, but also the material is given for a study of Bach's vocal and harmonic treatment of texts, and, in the second volume of this set, of his orchestration. Incidentally, there is substantial material for the study of figured basses.

This work would be incomplete without the provision of a few words of historical comment regarding the tunes, hymns,† and translations. Much care has been exercised to secure translations that are faithful and yet of some poetic value. Those of Dr. Emanuel Cronenwett (1841-1931), an Ohio-Pennsylvania Lutheran pastor, are of special interest in this country. Other Bach settings of the same melody, often several in number, are listed in each instance, including the additional numbers in the 1784-1787 edition mentioned above.

Each chorale has its accompaniment, and the instruments are named in this book as they are given in the Bachgesellschaft Edition. In the simpler chorale settings the *Continuo* is usually identical with the vocal bass; occasional differences are indicated by smaller notes, either on the staff with the bass part or on a separate staff. It should be remembered that the *Continuo* was usually played on a *Violone*, as well as on the 16-foot organ stops, sounding an octave lower than written. Without this consideration, the real bass is not always clearly understood. In earlier editions of the chorales, usually reduced to four parts, there was frequent confusion of the vocal bass with the *Continuo*. All the figured basses are given here as found in the Bachgesellschaft Edition. The student should bear in mind that Bach's use of these figures differed slightly at times from the modern application. For instance, the use of 7♭ where 7♮ is meant was comparatively frequent. Examples of this may be seen in Chorales 63 and 69. At least one example of each chorale melody which Bach harmonized in his compositions will be found in this compilation.

For the information of organ students and others

---

* In addition to the more or less complete editions of the chorales mentioned above, numerous collections containing from ten to one hundred chorales have been issued by various music publishers. In a large measure, they all have one or another of the weaknesses described in the preceding paragraphs.

† Throughout the notes in this edition, the word "hymn" refers to the text or words of the chorale, as contrasted with the tune or melody. This is the current usage in the literature of hymnology.

who use instrumental music based on chorale themes, reference has been made to Bach's organ pieces built about the melodies here given.

The chorales are arranged in four groups: Nos. 1-34, 35-68, 69-91, and 92-120. The first three groups appear in this volume, and the fourth appears in Volume II of this edition. Each group is arranged alphabetically; and the four groups, as units, stand in a progressive order of difficulty. It may be well to suggest to the student that he might wisely begin with but two voices at a time. Soprano and bass should preferably be taken first, then alto and bass, and then tenor and bass, until some familiarity with the C-clefs is obtained.

The vocal score in modern clefs brings this music within the reach of choruses. The accompanying orchestral parts for the chorales in Book II make it also practicable for combined choral and orchestral performance. The orchestration first given in each case is Bach's; where changes for modern wind in-struments seem desirable, the indications are to be regarded as merely suggested. The very high Horn and Trumpet parts are given in the orchestral parts in two ways: first, in their original form, as Bach wrote them; and then, transcribed for another instrument. The most practical instrument, perhaps, will be the Clarinet; but, where it seems foreign to the tone-color desired, a Fluegel-Horn might be considered.

The compilation of this collection would have been an impossibility without the Bachgesellschaft Edition and the distinguished labors of Johannes Zahn, Albert Schweitzer, Charles Sanford Terry, and John Julian, a list of whose works pertaining more or less directly to Bach is given on another page. The editors acknowledge with thanks the courtesy of the family of the late Dr. Emanuel Cronenwett for permission to use his translations.

CHARLES N. BOYD*
ALBERT RIEMENSCHNEIDER

* Unfortunately, Dr. Charles N. Boyd did not live to see this edition in print, having died April 24, 1937.

ESSENTIAL BIBLIOGRAPHY

John Julian, *A Dictionary of Hymnology*, reprint of second edition (New York: Charles Scribner's Sons: 1907)

C. Hubert H. Parry, *Johann Sebastian Bach* (New York: G. P. Putnam's Sons: 1909)

Albert Schweitzer, *J. S. Bach*, English translation by Ernest Newman, two volumes (Leipzig and New York: Breitkopf & Härtel: 1911)

Philipp Spitta, *Johann Sebastian Bach*, English translation by Clara Bell and J. A. Fuller-Maitland, three volumes (London: Novello, Ewer & Co.; New York: H. W. Gray Co.: 1899)

Charles Sanford Terry, *Bach's Chorals*, the hymns and hymn-melodies of the

    (Vol. I) "Passions" and Oratorios (1915)
    (Vol. II) Cantatas and Motetts (1917)
    (Vol. III) Organ Works (1921)
    (Cambridge, Eng.: Cambridge University Press)

The Four-Part Chorals of J. S. Bach (London and New York: Oxford University Press: 1929)

Johannes Zahn, *Die Melodien der deutschen evangelischen Kirchenlieder*, six volumes (Gütersloh: C. Bertelsmann: 1889-1893)

CONTENTS

NOTES ON THE CHORALES

1. ACH GOTT, VOM HIMMEL SIEH' DAREIN

Martin Luther's first hymns were written in 1523. A year later, the first Lutheran hymnal appeared, entitled *Etlich Christlich lider Lobgesang, und Psalm* and published at Wittenberg. Among the eight songs in this booklet was the hymn "Ach Gott, vom Himmel sieh' darein", which is Luther's paraphrase of Psalm 12. A facsimile of the page containing this hymn may be seen on page lxix of the preface to the "Historical Edition" of *Hymns Ancient and Modern* (London: Clowes: 1909).

The tune set to the hymn in the 1524 book was not the one used here, which appeared in another book of the same year, the Erfurt *Enchiridion*, a collection of 25 songs, 18 of which were made by Luther.

Bach made other chorale harmonizations of this melody: in Cantata 2, to the words "Das wollst du Gott bewahren rein"; and in Cantata 77, to "Du stellst, mein Jesu, selber dich". It is also No. 253 in the Edition of 1786.

In the present setting the instruments simply double the voice parts, the soprano being assigned to *Violino I*, the alto to *Violino II*, the tenor to *Viola*, and the bass to the *Continuo* instruments.

The words for which Bach made this setting are the first stanza of a hymn attributed to David Denicke, which was published in 1646 to the melody here used. The English translation* has been made for this edition by Charles N. Boyd.

2. ACH GOTT, WIE MANCHES HERZELEID

The melody used here was published in 1625 in *As hymnodus sacer* (Leipzig) as a setting to Martin Behm's hymn "Herr Jesu Christ, mein's Lebens Licht". Five years later it was associated with the present hymn. Bach made other chorale-harmonizations of this melody: in Cantata 3, where it is given with the words "Wie schwerlich lässt sich Fleisch und Blut" (interwoven with recitatives for S., A., T., and B.); and in Cantata 153, with the words "Drum will ich, weil ich lebe noch".

The instrumentation for the present setting assigns the parts as follows: soprano to *Violino I, Corno*, and *Oboi d'amore I & II*; alto to *Violino II*; tenor to *Viola*; and bass to the *Continuo* instruments.

This hymn was published in Martin Moller's *Meditationes Sanctorum Patrum* (Görlitz: 1587) under the heading "A consoling prayer wherewith a troubled soul, amid all the crosses and tribulations of these last troublous times, can sweetly comfort itself and longingly delight itself in the Sweet Name of Jesus Christ. From the ancient hymn 'Jesu dulcis memoria'." The authorship of the revision from the Latin is attributed by some to Moller and by others to Conrad Hojer. The English version, by J. C. Jacobi, was published in 1722.

3. AUF MEINEN LIEBEN GOTT

This melody appears in numerous forms in the first third of the seventeenth century. Terry cites a secular song of 1574, "Venus du und dein Kind", as having been associated with this tune. In 1609 the melody was published in Vulpius's *Ein schön geistlich Gesangbuch* (Jena), with this hymn.

Bach used this melody in several of his cantatas besides No. 188. In No. 5 it is set to "Wo soll ich fliehen hin" and to "Führ' auch mein Herz und Sinn"; in No. 89 it is set to "Mir mangelt zwar sehr viel"; and in No. 136 it is set, with violin obbligato, to "Dein Blut, der edle Saft". Bach also wrote two chorale-preludes on this melody under the title "Wo soll ich fliehen hin".

The instrumentation for Cantata 188 is as follows: *Oboe, Violini I & II, Viola, Violoncello, Organo obbligato*, and *Continuo*. Since the score does not indicate which instruments were assigned to play for the singing of the chorale, it may be supposed that the instruments were allotted to the vocal parts in the usual manner. The *Continuo* was not figured.

This hymn of trust in God was published in *Geistliche Psalmen* (Nürnberg: 1607). The identity of its author is uncertain, but it is usually attributed to Sigismund Weingärtner. The English translation is by J. C. Jacobi, and was published in 1722.

4. AUS TIEFER NOTH SCHREI ICH ZU DIR

Luther made his transcription of Psalm 130 in 1523. In the following year it was published twice with this melody, which may be attributed to Luther himself, in the *Geystliche gesangk Buchleyn* (Wittenberg), and in the Erfurt *Enchiridion*. Also in 1524 the hymn was published to another tune, in a third book.

Bach's choral works, so far as they survive, do not contain another harmonization of this melody. Two of his chorale-preludes for organ are written on it: one with double pedal and the *cantus firmus* in the upper pedal, the other in four-part imitative writing.

The instrumentation indicated by Bach in this setting is as follows: for the soprano, *Oboi I & II*,

* The English texts will be found in the close-score versions (pp. 78-127).

Violino I, and *Trombone I;* for the alto, *Violino II* and *Trombone II;* for the tenor, *Viola* and *Trombone III;* and for the bass, *Trombone IV* and *Continuo.*

The text of this setting is the fifth stanza of Luther's hymn. The hymn was sung at Luther's funeral in Wittenberg, on February 20, 1546. The English translation is by Arthur Tozer Russell, and was published in 1851.

5. CHRIST IST ERSTANDEN

The melody used here was derived from the last part of an Easter song which had been popular since the thirteenth century. Its first appearance in print seems to have been in 1513. Many versions arose, varying in length from five to eleven stanzas: in Luther's time a three-stanza form was favored. The complete melody is in Klug's *Geistliche Lieder zu Wittemberg* (Wittenberg: 1535). Of it Luther said, "After a time one tires of singing all other hymns, but the 'Christ ist erstanden' one can always sing again".

The only other chorale harmonization of this melody among Bach's works is No. 197 in the Edition of 1786, which is a long setting covering the three stanzas. The triumphant chorale-prelude on this melody in Bach's *Orgelbüchlein* also follows the three-stanza form.

No instrumentation is indicated in the score of this chorale, but the cantata calls for *Tromba, Oboi I & II, Fagotto, Violini I & II, Viola,* and *Continuo.* The *Continuo* is not figured.

The words of the chorale here given are the third stanza. The translation is by Dr. Charles N. Boyd.

6. CHRIST LAG IN TODESBANDEN

This hymn by Martin Luther was published twice in 1524, with the title "The hymn 'Christ ist erstanden' improved". Actually, Luther had taken parts of earlier Latin hymns, and added much of his own. The two books in which his hymn appeared were Johann Walther's *Geystliche gesangk Buchleyn* (Wittenberg) and the Erfurt *Enchiridion.* For both books Walther provided what appears to be versions of an older melody. The form used here by Bach seems to derive from the Wittenberg version.

Bach used this melody in his Cantata 158, where it is set to the words "Hier ist das rechte Osterlamm". It is also found as No. 15 in the Edition of 1784, as No. 261 in the Edition of 1786, and as No. 370 in the Edition of 1787. One of the preludes in the *Orgelbüchlein,* and two among the other chorale-preludes, are based on this melody. All three of the organ pieces are meditative in character. Schweitzer (II, 63)

suggests that the bass pattern in one of these preludes calls to mind "the heavy bonds of death".

As Cantata 4, based upon this melody, is one of the best examples of the so-called chorale cantatas, it should be mentioned at this point. The whole cantata is a set of chorale variations in which each movement, setting one stanza of the hymn, receives a different treatment, with the chorale melody as a basis. The cantata ends with the usual statement of the chorale itself in four parts.

The instrumentation of this chorale gives the soprano to *Violini I & II* and *Cornetto,* the alto to *Viola I* and *Trombone I,* the tenor to *Viola II* and *Trombone II,* and the bass to *Trombone III* and *Continuo* (not figured).

The English version is by Charles N. Boyd.

7. CHRISTUS, DER UNS SELIG MACHT

The melody used for this hymn has been traced back to that used for Michael Weisse's German version of the Latin "Patris sapientia, veritas divina", in *Ein New Gesengbuchlen* (Jungen Buntzel: 1531), by way of Seth Calvisius's *Harmonia Cantionum ecclesiasticarum* (Leipzig: 1598).

This melody was used again in the "St. John Passion", to the words "O hilf, Christe, Gottes Sohn". There are also two duplicate harmonizations of it: No. 198 in the Edition of 1786 and No. 306 in the Edition of 1787. The chorale-prelude setting of this melody in the *Orgelbüchlein* takes the form of a canon in the octave.

The instrumentation for the present use of this chorale is as follows: soprano, *Flauti traversi I & II, Oboe I,* and *Violino I;* alto, *Oboe II* and *Violino II;* tenor, *Viola;* and bass, *Organo e Continuo.*

The English version of Weisse's hymn has been made by Albert Riemenschneider for this edition.

8. DU FRIEDEFÜRST, HERR JESU CHRIST

The melody, which is probably by Bartholomäus Gesius, appeared in his *Geistliche deutsche Lieder* (Frankfurt a. O.: 1601), with this hymn.

Another Bach harmonization of this melody is found in Cantata 116, to the words "Erleucht' auch unsern Sinn und Herz".

The instrumentation for the present setting is as follows: soprano, *Corno da tirarsi, Flauto traverso, Oboe d'amore I,* and *Violino I;* alto, *Oboe d'amore II* and *Violino II;* tenor, *Viola;* and bass, *Organo e Continuo.*

The text is from a hymn by Jakob Ebert, "In Time of War, a prayer for peace". The English translation is by J. C. Jacobi, and appeared in 1722.

9. DU, O SCHÖNES WELTGEBÄUDE

This melody by Johann Crüger was published with this hymn in his *Geistliche Kirchen-Melodien* (Leipzig: 1649).

Another harmonization by Bach is found in the Edition of 1785 as No. 137.

The instrumentation here used assigns to the soprano *Oboi I & II* and *Violino I*, to the alto *Violino II*, to the tenor *Taille* and *Viola*, and to the bass *Continuo* (unfigured).

The hymn, by Johann Franck, began originally "Du geballtes Weltgebäude". The English translation has been made by Charles N. Boyd for this edition.

10. ERSCHIENEN IST DER HERRLICH' TAG

Nicolaus Herman (1485-1561) was the author of the hymn and composer of the melody, both appearing together in *Die Sontags Euangelia uber das gantze Jar* (Wittenberg: 1560).

Bach made another harmonization of this melody for Cantata 145, where it is set to the words "Drum wir auch billig fröhlich sein". The chorale-prelude on this tune in the *Orgelbüchlein* is a canon in the octave, between soprano and bass.

The instrumentation for the present setting is as follows: soprano, *Corno da tirarsi*, *Flauto traverso*, *Oboe d'amore I*, and *Violino I*; alto, *Oboe d'amore II* and *Violino II*; tenor, *Viola*; and bass, *Organo e Continuo*.

The translation of the hymn, by Arthur Tozer Russell, was published in 1851.

11. FREU' DICH SEHR, O MEINE SEELE

The original of this melody seems to be the work of Louis Bourgeois, first published in his *Psalms* (1542) to a French version of Psalm 42, "Ainsi qu'on oit". What appears to be a derivative of this melody was published with the text "Freu' dich sehr" in Christopher Demantius's *Threnodiae, Das ist: Ausserlesene Trostreiche Begräbnuss Gesänge* (Freiberg: 1620).

Bach made abundant use of this melody in his cantatas. In No. 19 it is set to the words "Lass dein' Engel mit mir fahren" (here with an independent instrumentation for three Trumpets, two Oboes, *Taille*, Strings, and *Continuo*), in No. 25 to "Ich will alle meine Tage", in No. 30 to "Eine Stimme lässt sich hören" (No. 72 in this collection), in No. 32 to "Mein Gott, öffne mir die Pforten" (this setting), in No. 39 to "Selig sind, die aus Erbarmen", in No. 70 to "Freu' dich sehr, o meine Seele", and in No. 194 to "Heil'ger Geist in's Himmels Throne". It is also found as No. 297 in the Edition of 1787.

The instrumentation here given is as follows: soprano, *Oboe* and *Violino I*; alto, *Violino II*; tenor, *Viola*; and bass, *Continuo* (unfigured).

This hymn for the dying has been attributed to several authors. It seems to be the work of Paul Gerhardt. The English translation has been made by Charles N. Boyd for this edition.

12. GELOBET SEIST DU, JESU CHRIST

The Latin sequence "Grates nunc omnes reddamus Domino Deo", with its melody, is responsible for the present combination of hymn and tune. The Latin sequence has been traced back to the eleventh century, and a German version dates from as early as 1370. In the latter there was but one stanza. Luther added six more of his own; and the complete hymn, with this melody, was published in Johann Walther's *Geystliche gesangk Buchleyn* (Wittenberg: 1524). The tune is apparently an adaptation of the one which belonged to the Latin original.

Bach used this melody three times to the words "Das hat er Alles uns gethan" (the seventh stanza of Luther's hymn): in Cantata 64, in Cantata 91 (with two Horns and Timpani *obbligati*), and in the "Christmas Oratorio". A setting is also found as No. 287 in the Edition of 1787.

Bach based four chorale-preludes on this tune. The one in the *Orgelbüchlein* is short, with very little decoration of the melody. In the other sets, one prelude is in chorale form, with florid interludes; the second is a fughetta; and the third is a contrapuntal setting of the melody in its plainest form.

The instrumentation here specified is as follows: soprano, *Violino I* and *Cornetto*; alto, *Violino II* and *Trombone I*; tenor, *Viola* and *Trombone II*; and bass, *Organo e Continuo* (unfigured) and *Trombone III*.

The English translation of this stanza is by Richard Massie.

13. HERR CHRIST, DER EIN'GE GOTTES-SOHN

The hymn and the melody were published together twice in 1524: in the Erfurt *Enchiridion* and in Walther's *Geystliche gesangk Buchleyn* (Wittenberg). The melody has a strong likeness to that of a secular song "Ich hört ein Fräulein klagen", which, though not published until later, may be older than the chorale melody.

Bach made two other harmonizations of this melody, to the words "Ertödt' uns durch dein' Güte": in Cantata 22 (a setting with interludes, accompanied by Oboe, Strings, and *Continuo*) and in Cantata 164. The *Orgelbüchlein* contains a prelude on this melody, and there is also a fughetta on it among the other chorale-preludes.

The instrumentation in the present instance is as follows: soprano, *Corno, Oboi I & II*, and *Violino I;* alto, *Violino II;* tenor, *Viola;* and bass, *Continuo.*

Elisabethe Cruciger, whose husband was a pupil and friend of Luther, wrote this Christmas hymn, the only one of her authorship that is known. The English translation is a modernized version of that made by Bishop Miles Coverdale in 1539.

14-18. HERZLICH THUT MICH VERLANGEN

It has been pointed out in the Preface that Bach seldom used the same harmonization of a chorale for different purposes. His harmonizations are dictated largely by two considerations: first, the words themselves; and, second, the situation in which the chorale is used. Both of these factors are important; and, in order to enter into the spirit of any chorale from one of his major choral works, it is necessary to consider them both.

The Hassler melody upon which this chorale is based seems to have been a favorite of Bach's, as he used it no less than ten times. Its five appearances in the "St. Matthew Passion" offer a unique opportunity to study Bach's manner of treating this melody.

In the first two appearances of the chorale in the "St. Matthew Passion", the same harmonization is used, the only difference being that the second is sung a half-step lower than the first. This fact has a significance that is explained in the recitative that separates them:

"Peter answered and said unto Him, 'Though all men shall be offended because of Thee, yet will I never be offended'.

Jesus said to him, 'Verily I say unto thee that this night, before the cock crow, thou shalt deny Me thrice'.

Peter said unto Him, 'Though I should die with Thee, yet will I not deny Thee'. Likewise said all the disciples".

The element of uncertainty which the statement of the Savior produces is symbolized in this change of key.

An especially interesting feature of all these harmonizations is the seeming strife between major and minor modes, and the presence of a considerable modal element. At times the chorale begins in minor and ends in major; or it may open in one key and end in another. These features, together with the relation of words and harmonies, and some descriptive details of voice-leading, have led the editors to present all five of the versions from the "St. Matthew Passion" in order to offer an opportunity for comparative study.

This melody by Hans Leo Hassler was originally a secular song, published to the words "Mein G'müt ist mir verwirret" in his *Lustgarten Neuer Teutscher Gesäng* (Nürnberg: 1601). It also appeared in *Harmoniae sacrae* (Görlitz: 1613) associated with Christoph Knoll's hymn "Herzlich thut mich verlangen"; and in Crüger's *Praxis Pietatis Melica* (Frankfurt: 1656) it was published with the hymn with which it is often associated, Paul Gerhardt's "O Haupt voll Blut und Wunden".

There are many other Bach harmonizations of this melody. It is used five times in the "St. Matthew Passion", this being the first, followed by No. 23 "Ich will hier bei dir stehen", No. 53 "Befiehl du deine Wege", No. 63 "O Haupt voll Blut und Wunden", and No. 72 "Wenn ich einmal soll scheiden". It occurs twice in the "Christmas Oratorio": to "Wie soll ich dich empfangen" and to "Nun seid ihr wohl gerochen", the latter with accompaniment for *Trombe I, II, & III, Timpani, Oboi I & II, Violini I & II, Viola, Organo,* and *Continuo,* with interludes. In Cantata 135 it is set to "Ehr' sei in's Himmels Throne", in Cantata 153 to "Und obgleich alle Teufel", and in Cantata 161 to "Der Leib zwar in der Erden". The latter, with accompaniment of two Flutes, Strings, and *Continuo,* is No. 96 in the present collection. Other harmonizations are No. 270 in the Edition of 1786, and Nos. 285 and 366 in the Edition of 1787. A note on Bach's use of this melody for the organ chorale-prelude is found with No. 96 of the present collection.

The instrumentation for the five appearances in the "St. Matthew Passion" is as follows: soprano, *Flauti traversi I & II, Oboi I & II,* and *Violino I;* alto, *Violino II;* tenor, *Viola;* and bass, *Organo e Continuo.* The only exception to this instrumentation is in the second appearance (No. 23) where *Flauti traversi I & II* are not designated.

Knoll's hymn for the dying is said to have been written during a pestilence in 1599, and first printed at Görlitz in 1605. The English translations of Nos. 14, 16, 17, and 18 are by John S. Dwight, and the translation of No. 15 is by Dr. James W. Alexander.

19. HERZLIEBSTER JESU, WAS·HAST DU VERBROCHEN

This melody, with a setting in four-part harmony, was composed by Johann Crüger for Heermann's hymn, and the combination was published in the

Newes vollkömliches Gesangbuch (Berlin: 1640).

In the "St. Matthew Passion", Bach sets this melody also to the words "Was ist die Ursach' aller solcher Plagen?" and to "Wie wunderbarlich ist doch diese Strafe!"; and in the "St. John Passion" he sets it to "O grosse Lieb', o Lieb' ohn' alle Maasse" and to "Ach, grosser König, gross zu allen Zeiten".

The accompaniment for the present setting is assigned as follows: soprano, *Violino I, Flauti traversi,* and *Oboi*; alto, *Violino II*; tenor, *Viola*; and bass *Organo e Continuo.*

Johann Heermann's Passiontide hymn "Herzliebster Jesu, was hast du verbrochen" is based on No. vii of the *Meditationes* of St. Augustine, a collection in which this meditation is credited to St. Anselm. The English translation is slightly altered from that made by Catherine Winkworth for her *Lyra Germanica* (1855).

20. JESU LEIDEN, PEIN UND TOD

The history of this melody begins with its association in 1609 with a hymn by Petrus Herbert, "Jesu Kreuz, Leiden und Pein"; Melchior Vulpius is given as the composer. In the form used by Bach, the melody appeared with the present hymn in Gottfried Vopelius's *New Leipziger Gesangbuch* (Leipzig: 1682).

Bach used this melody again in the "St. John Passion", to the words "Er nahm alles wohl in Acht" and "Jesu, der du warest todt" (with bass solo); and he used it in Cantata 159 to "Jesus, deine Passion".

For the present setting the instrumentation is as follows: soprano, *Flauti traversi I & II, Oboe I,* and *Violino I*; alto, *Oboe II* and *Violino II*; tenor, *Viola*; and bass, *Organo e Continuo.*

This is the tenth stanza of a Passiontide hymn by Paul Stockmann. The English translation was made especially for this edition by Albert Riemenschneider.

21. JESUS, MEINE ZUVERSICHT

Two versions of this melody were published in 1653, in Berlin. One was in Johann Crüger's *Praxis Pietatis Melica,* and the other was in Christoph Runge's *Geistliche Lieder und Psalmen.* In neither case was the name of the composer given. But fifteen years later, Crüger's initials were attached to the melody; and it is therefore supposed that he was either the composer or the arranger.

Another harmonization of this melody is No. 175 in the Edition of 1785. It is not used elsewhere in the cantatas. One of the shortest of Bach's chorale-preludes for the organ is based on this melody.

No instrumentation for this chorale is indicated in the score, but the following instruments are used in the cantata: *Tromba, Flauto traverso, Oboi d'amorè I & II, Violini I & II, Viola,* and *Continuo.*

The words are the first stanza of Caspar Neumann's Easter hymn "Auf, mein Herz", which appeared, set to this melody, in *Vollständige Kirchen- und Haus-Musik* (Breslau: c. 1700). The English translation is by Charles N. Boyd.

22. LIEBSTER IMMANUEL, HERZOG DER FROMMEN

According to Zahn and others, it is hard to determine whether this melody was religious or secular in its origin and early association. It is found, marked as a *Courant,* in a book of 54 dances in tablature, which the owner inscribed as having been bought March 21, 1681. It appeared with the words of this hymn, however, in the *Himmels-Lust und Welt-Unlust* (Jena: 1679) of Ahashuerus Fritzsch, to whom these words are often ascribed. A second form, with the words "Schönster Immanuel", appeared in the *Geistreiches Gesang-Buch* (Darmstadt: 1698). Many variants of the tune became common.

This appears to be the only existing harmonization by Bach of this melody.

The instrumentation is as follows: soprano, *Flauti traversi I & II (in 8va), Oboi d'amore I & II,* and *Violino I*; alto, *Violino II*; tenor, *Viola*; and bass, *Continuo* (unfigured).

The English translation is by Albert Riemenschneider.

23. LOBT GOTT, IHR CHRISTEN ALLE GLEICH

This melody was first published in 1554 on a single sheet, to the words:

> Kommt her, ihr lieben Schwesterlein,
> An diesen Abendtanz;
> Lasst uns ein geistlichs Liedelein
> Singen um einen Kranz.

Both words and music were by Nicolaus Herman, who afterwards used the melody for his hymn "Lobt Gott, ihr Christen alle gleich", which was printed in his *Die Sontags Euangelia uber das gantze Jar* (Wittenberg: 1560).

Bach made other harmonizations of this melody for "Nun danket all' und bringet Ehr' " (with obbligati consisting of *Corni I & II* and *Timpani*) in Cantata 195; and as No. 276 in the Edition of 1786 and No. 341 in the Edition of 1787. He also based two animated chorale-preludes for organ (one in the *Orgelbüchlein*) on this melody.

The instrumentation here specified is as follows: soprano, *Flauto traverso*, *Oboe d'amore*, and *Violino I*; alto, *Violino II*; tenor, *Viola*; and bass, *Continuo* (unfigured).

The English translation of Herman's Christmas hymn was made by the Rev. Emanuel Cronenwett, in 1880.

24. MACH'S MIT MIR, GOTT, NACH DEINER GÜT'

This melody and its hymn, both by Johann Hermann Schein, were published on a single sheet at Leipzig in 1628, as a memorial on the death of Margaret Werner. Later both hymn and tune were included in hymn collections.

Other harmonizations by Bach are in Cantata 139, to the words "Dahero Trotz der Höllen Heer!", and in the Edition of 1784, as No. 44.

The instrumentation for this setting is as follows: soprano, *Flauti traversi I & II*, *Oboi I & II*, and *Violino I*; alto, *Violino II*; tenor, *Viola*; and bass, *Organo e Continuo*.

The English translation was made by Charles N. Boyd for this edition.

25. MEINE SEEL' ERHEBT DEN HERREN

The Gregorian melody known as *Tonus peregrinus*, a combination of Modes I and VIII, has long been used for the psalm "In exitu Israel"; and the melody that Bach used here is based upon it. An interesting use of this melody is also found in Bach's great Latin *Magnificat* in D, where the setting of "Suscepit Israel" for three women's voices and *Continuo* also includes this melody in obbligato form for *Oboi I & II all' unisono*. In the E-flat version of this *Magnificat*, this same melody was given to the *Tromba*. Other Bach harmonizations of this melody are No. 130 in the Edition of 1785 and No. 319 in the Edition of 1787. There is also a fugue among the chorale-preludes.

In Cantata 10 Bach used this melody as an obbligato for *Tromba* and *Oboi I & II*, in unison, to an alto and tenor duet "Er denket der Barmherzigkeit". This duet appears as an organ solo, entitled "Meine Seele erhebt den Herren", the fourth of the six Schübler Chorales, which are transcriptions of various movements from Bach choral works.

The instruments are assigned as follows: to soprano, *Tromba*, *Oboi I & II*, and *Violino I*; to alto, *Violino II*; to tenor, *Viola*; and to bass, *Continuo*.

26. NUN KOMM, DER HEIDEN HEILAND

Luther's Christmas hymn "Nun komm, der Heiden Heiland", is a German version of the Latin "Veni Redemptor gentium", which is attributed to St. Ambrose (340-397). The melody, probably adapted by Johann Walther, was twice printed in 1524: in the Erfurt *Enchiridion* and in Walther's *Geystliche gesangk Buchleyn*.

Bach made another harmonization of this melody, to the same words (which are the eighth stanza of the hymn), in Cantata 36. He wrote five organ-preludes on the melody, one in the *Orgelbüchlein*, three in the set of *Eighteen Chorales*.

The instruments are assigned in this setting as follows: soprano, *Corno*, *Oboi I & II*, and *Violino I*; alto, *Violino II*; tenor, *Viola*; and bass, *Continuo*.

The translation is by Albert Riemenschneider.

27. O EWIGKEIT, DU DONNERWORT

Johann Rist (1607-1667) is said to have written some 680 hymns, many of which had wide use in Germany. His "Wach auf, mein Geist, erhebe dich", was published with the original form of the present melody, composed by Johann Schop, in *Himlischer Lieder* (1642). This hymn was in the same collection, with another melody by Schop. The association of the present melody with "O Ewigkeit, du Donnerwort" did not begin until *Praxis Pietatis Melica* (Berlin: 1653). For that collection Johann Crüger made a revision of the original melody.

Bach also used the present harmonization for "So lang ein Gott im Himmel lebt", in Cantata 20. There is another harmonization as No. 274 in the Edition of 1786. It also appears in the Note-Book of Anna Magdalena Bach as No. 42 of that set.

The instrumentation here used is as follows: soprano, *Tromba da tirarsi*, *Oboi I & II*, and *Violino I*; alto, *Oboe III* and *Violino II*; tenor, *Viola*; and bass, *Continuo*.

The English translation was made by J. C. Jacobi in 1722.

28. PREISE, JERUSALEM, DEN HERRN (HERR GOTT, DICH LOBEN WIR)

As the words here sung are taken from Luther's German version of the "Te Deum", the melodic phrases also derive from the ancient Latin plainsong tune. The combination was published in Joseph Klug's *Geistliche Lieder* (Wittenberg: 1535). Zahn (under No. 8652) thinks that it perhaps appeared in the lost first edition of that book, published in 1529. The *Amen* was added by Bach.

A long setting of this chorale, evidently for liturgical use, is found as No. 205 in the Edition of 1786.

No instrumentation of this chorale is indicated in the score. The instrumentation of the cantata is unusually rich, consisting of *Trombe I, II, III, & IV, Timpani, Flauti I & II, Oboi I, II, & III, Oboi da caccia I & II, Violini I & II, Viola,* and *Continuo* (unfigured). The cantata was written for the inauguration of the Leipzig Town Council, 1723.

The English version is a revision of the translation by Richard Massie.

29. PUER NATUS IN BETHLEHEM

The Latin hymn "Puer natus in Bethlehem" and the German version "Ein Kind geborn zu Bethlehem" appeared with an old melody in Joseph Klug's *Geistliche Lieder* (Wittenberg: 1543). Ten years later the words appeared with another melody in Lucas Lossius's *Psalmodia* (Nürnberg); but the later melody, which is the one used here, is without doubt the discant for the earlier melody. The earlier one was used in contemporary settings as a *cantus firmus* in the tenor.

This is the only harmonization by Bach that has been preserved. The striking pictorial figure of the wise men bowing before the Savior is prominent in this setting of the chorale; in the prelude on this melody in the *Orgelbüchlein* this figure has received further development. A comparison of the chorale and chorale-prelude is very interesting.

In the score, *Flauti I & II* are written out an octave higher than the soprano part. *Oboe da caccia I* duplicates the alto, and *Oboe da caccia II* the tenor. Both are written out on separate staves. The *Continuo* was not figured. In addition to the above instruments, the cantata is scored for *Corni I & II, Violini I & II,* and *Viola.*

The English version was made by H. M. MacGill.

30. VALET WILL ICH DIR GEBEN

"Valet will ich dir geben" was, according to a broadsheet printed at Leipzig in 1614, "a hymn of consolation in which a pious heart bids farewell (*Valet*) to this world, written by Valerius Herberger, preacher at the *Kripplein Christi*". On the broadsheet were two melodies written for the hymn by Melchior Teschner, both with a five-part setting. The second melody has not survived in common use, but the first is still found in many hymnals under the name of "St. Theodulph".

Another Bach harmonization of this melody is found in the Edition of 1784 as No. 24, and two of the organ chorale-preludes are based on it.

The instruments are assigned as follows in the present setting: soprano, *Flauti traversi I & II, Oboi I & II,* and *Violino I;* alto, *Violino II;* tenor, *Viola;* and bass, *Organo e Continuo.*

The English version of the third stanza of Herberger's hymn is by Catherine Winkworth, and was published in 1863.

31. VOM HIMMEL HOCH, DA KOMM' ICH HER

Luther's Christmas song for children, "Vom Himmel hoch da komm' ich her", was published in Valentin Schumann's *Geistliche lieder auffs new gebessert* (Leipzig: 1539). The melody is often attributed to Luther himself; Winterfeld thought it of secular origin, and Weber considered it an adaptation from Gregorian sources. Eventually this melody completely displaced another with which the hymn had first appeared four years previously.

Other settings by Bach of this melody are two from the "Christmas Oratorio", No. 23, to the words "Wir singen dir in deinem Heer" (with interludes), and No. 9, to "Ach, mein herzliebes Jesulein" (this with obbligato parts for *Trombe I, II, & III,* and *Timpani*), and one associated with the E-flat version of the *Magnificat,* given as No. 105 in this collection.

For Bach's organ music on this melody, see the note on No. 105.

The translation is by Albert Riemenschneider.

32. WARUM SOLLT' ICH MICH DENN GRÄMEN

Julian's *Dictionary of Hymnology* ranks Paulus Gerhardt next to Luther as the most gifted and popular hymn-writer of the Lutheran Church. His hymn "Warum sollt' ich mich denn grämen" was published in a volume of his *Geistliche Andachten* (Berlin: 1666). The hymn had appeared as early as 1653 with other melodies, but this one, by Johann Georg Ebeling, was widely used in varying versions. The one that Bach adopted was based on the melody as found in Daniel Vetter's *Musicalische Kirchen- und Hauss-Ergötzlichkeit* (Leipzig: 1713).

Another Bach harmonization of this chorale is found as No. 356 in the Edition of 1787.

The instrumentation for the present setting is as follows: soprano, *Flauti traversi I & II* (in *8va*), *Oboi I & II,* and *Violino I;* alto, *Violino II;* tenor, *Viola;* and bass, *Organo e Continuo.*

The English translation of this, the fifteenth and last, stanza of Gerhardt's hymn is by Catherine Winkworth.

33. WAS GOTT THUT, DAS IST WOHLGETHAN

This melody was published, anonymously, in the *Nürnbergisches Gesang-Buch* of 1690. The composer is not known. Severus Gastorius and Johann Pachelbel have been mentioned in connection with it; but since a book of 1693 mentions the melody as well-known, Zahn is inclined to think it older than 1690.

Bach set this melody several times. It is found in the following: Cantata 69 (variant) with the words "Was Gott thut, das ist wohlgethan, dabei will ich verbleiben"; Cantata 75, with *Oboi I & II* and Strings *obbligati*, with interludes, to the words "Was Gott thut, das its wohlgethan! Muss ich den Kelch gleich schmecken"; Cantata 98, with free String *obbligato* and interludes, to the words "Was Gott thut, das ist wohlgethan, es bleibt gerecht sein Wille"; Cantata 99, with *Flauto traverso (in 8va)*, *Oboe d'amore*, *Corno*, Strings, and *Continuo*, to the words "Was Gott thut, das ist wohlgethan, dabei will ich verbleiben" (the opening chorus of Cantata 99 is also a chorale fantasy based upon the melody); Cantata 100, with *Corni I & II, Timpani, Flauto traverso, Oboe d'amore*, Strings, Organ, and *Continuo*, with interludes, to the words "Was Gott thut, das ist wohlgethan, dabei will ich verbleiben" (the opening chorus of Cantata 100 is also based upon the melody). A setting from Cantata 12 is found as No. 117 of the present collection, and another is No. 114, one of the Wedding Chorales. Still another harmonization is No. 292 in the Edition of 1787.

The cantata from which this chorale is taken, "Nimm, was dein ist, und gehe hin", is of the motet type. The instrumentation is indicated in only two of the numbers: an aria with Strings and *Continuo*, and a second aria with *Oboe d'amore* and *Continuo*. No figures were marked for the *Continuo*.

This hymn of consolation is by Samuel Rodigast, probably written in 1675. The English translation was made by the Rev. Emanuel Cronenwett in 1878.

34. WER NUR DEN LIEBEN GOTT LÄSST WALTEN

Georg Neumark (1621-1681) had an interesting personal history, which has often been related, and left a number of hymns and other literary productions; but he will probably be remembered best by this hymn, the melody of which is also his. They were published together in his *Fortgepflantzter Musikalisch-Poetischer Lustwald* (Jena: 1657).

Bach used this melody in the following cantatas: No. 27, to "Wer weiss wie nahe mir mein Ende", with accompaniment of *Corno I, Oboi I & II*, Strings, and *Continuo*, with interludes and recitative; No. 84, to "Ich leb' indess in dir vergnüget"; No. 88, to "Sing', bet' und geh' auf Gottes Wegen"; No. 166, to "Wer weiss, wie nahe mir mein Ende?"; No. 179, to "Ich armer Mensch, ich armer Sünder"; and No. 197, the Wedding Cantata, to "So wandelt froh auf Gottes Wegen". It appears further as No. 146 in the Edition of 1785.

In addition to the setting in the *Orgelbüchlein*, Bach wrote three other preludes on this melody.

The instrumentation used for the present setting assigns *Oboi I & II* and *Violino I* to the soprano; *Violino II* to the alto; *Viola* to the tenor; and *Continuo* to the bass.

The translation, by Catherine Winkworth, was published in 1863.

35. ACH, GOTT UND HERR

The first appearance of this melody seems to have been in *As hymnodus sacer* (Leipzig: 1625), where it is set to this hymn. Thirty years later the melody, more closely approximating the present form, was assigned to the same hymn in Christoph Peter's *Andachts Zymbeln Oder andächtige und geistreiche . . . Lieder* (Freiberg: 1655).

Another harmonization by J. S. Bach of this melody is No. 40 in the Edition of 1784.

The instrumentation specified in Cantata 48 assigns, to the soprano, *Tromba, Oboi I & II*, and *Violino I*; to the alto, *Violino II*; to the tenor, *Viola*; and, to the bass, *Continuo* (unfigured).

Bach wrote three short chorale-preludes for organ on this melody.

The hymn is often attributed to Martin Rutilius (1550-1618); but Dr. Johann Major (or Gross) (1564-1654) seems more likely to have been the author. See the long account in Julian's *Dictionary*, pp. 982 and 1578. The English translation was made by Catherine Winkworth in the *Chorale Book for England* (1863).

36. ACH, LIEBEN CHRISTEN, SEID GETROST (WO GOTT DER HERR NICHT BEI UNS HÄLT)

The hymn ' Wo Gott der Herr nicht bei uns hält", by Justus Jonas, was first published in *Eyn Enchiridion* (Erfurt: 1524). In Klug's *Geistliche Lieder* (Wittenberg: 1535) it appeared with this melody. The hymn "Ach, lieben Christen, seid getrost", by Johannes Gigas (1514-1581), associated with several tunes, was first published in *Geistliche Lieder* (Frankfurt an der Oder: 1561) with this melody; and Bach thus preserved its original association.

Bach used the hymn "Wo Gott der Herr" in Cantata 178, with this melody, setting the seventh and eighth stanzas, "Die Feind' sind all' in deiner Hand" and "Den Himmel und auch die Erden", in chorale form. The fifth stanza, "Aufsperren sie den Rachen weit", contains a special *Continuo* part descriptive of the words. Recitatives are also interspersed between the verse lines. The opening chorus of Cantata 178 is also built upon this melody.

He set the melody to "Ach, lieben Christen" as it is found in the Edition of 1784, No. 31; it is also Nos. 284 and 335 in the Edition of 1787. In the cantata (of doubtful authenticity) "Siehe, es hat überwunden", it is set to the words "Lass deine Kirch' und unser Land" and "Zuletzt lass sie an unserm End' ".

For this chorale in Cantata 114, the instruments are assigned as follows: to the soprano, *Corno*, *Oboi I & II*, and *Violino I*; to the alto, *Violino II*; to the tenor, *Viola*; and, to the bass, *Continuo*.

The English translation is by J. C. Jacobi, and appeared in 1722.

37. ACH WIE FLÜCHTIG, ACH WIE NICHTIG

Though the melody may have been constructed from older melodies, the earliest known printing of it is in *Die Eitelkeit, Falschheit und Unbeständigkeit der Welt* (Coburg: 1652), where the melody and its setting, both by Michael Franck (1609-1667) are given. In 1661 a new version of the melody, with the hymn, appeared in two books: the *Neuvermehrtes vollständiges Gesangbuch* (Brunswick) and Crüger's *Praxis Pietatis Melica* (Berlin). The new version may have been made by Johann Crüger.

This is the only chorale-setting made by Bach, so far as is known.

The instrumentation in this instance is as follows: soprano, *Corno*, *Flauto traverso*, *Oboi I & II*, and *Violino I*; alto, *Oboe III* and *Violino II*; tenor, *Viola*; and bass, *Organo e Continuo*.

Referring to the use of this melody for one of the preludes in the *Orgelbüchlein*, Schweitzer calls attention to the fact that in both the chorale harmonization and the organ piece Bach uses scale passages to express the idea that life is like a cloud "that soon arises and soon has passed away".

The English translation, by Sir John Bowring, was published in 1825.

38. ALLE MENSCHEN MÜSSEN STERBEN

Zahn gives the melody, in the form that Bach has here used, as being found only in this cantata. Erk thought it a version of another melody. Terry, who in his *Bach's Chorals* quotes four melodies possibly involved, thinks that several melodies related to it were derived from a common source, which was perhaps older than a melody by Johann Rosenmüller, first printed on a separate sheet with this hymn in 1652; the melody that Bach used Terry thus regards as a variant of this.

Another Bach harmonization of a melody designated by this name is No. 153 in the Edition of 1785. The organ chorale in the *Orgelbüchlein*, known by

the same name, is based upon still another melody.

The instrumentation specified for this chorale is as follows: soprano, *Corno da tirarsi* and *Violino I*; alto, *Violino II*; tenor, *Viola*; and bass, *Fagotto* and *Continuo* (unfigured).

Speaking of the prelude in the *Orgelbüchlein*, Spitta mentions "the tender melancholy that lurks in it". Schweitzer says that "the melody of the hymn that speaks of the inevitability of death is . . . enveloped in a motive that is lit up by the coming glory".

This hymn by Johann Georg Albinus was written for the funeral of Paul von Henssberg, a merchant of Leipzig, and was sung in the setting by Rosenmüller, mentioned above, on June 1, 1652. The English translation (1856) is by Dr. Henry Mills, for many years a professor at Auburn Theological Seminary.

39. DAS NEUGEBOR'NE KINDELEIN

This hymn and tune were first published together in Melchior Vulpius's *Ein schön geistlich Gesangbuch* (Jena: 1609). The melody is attributed to Vulpius.

This appears to be Bach's only harmonization of the melody.

The instrumentation given in Cantata 122 for this chorale is as follows: soprano, *Oboe I* and *Violino I*; alto, *Oboe II* and *Violino II*; tenor, *Taille* and *Viola*; and bass, *Continuo* (unfigured).

The hymn, of which this is the fourth stanza, was written by Cyriacus Schneegass (1546-1597), a pastor noted for his musical ability. The anonymous translation here given is from *The Ohio Lutheran Hymnal* (1880).

40. DURCH ADAMS FALL IST GANZ VERDERBT

Lazarus Spengler's hymn of the Fall and Redemption, which Julian considers one of the most characteristic of its time, first appeared in the *Geystliche Gesangk Buchleyn* (Wittenberg: 1524). It was promptly taken up and used in other books, being provided with several different melodies and variants. The melody Bach used is from Joseph Klug's *Geistliche Lieder* (Wittenberg: 1535). Zahn quotes Böhme as his authority for saying that "Was wöll wir heben an" was sung to this melody at the Battle of Pavia in 1525.

Bach also set this melody, in Cantata 109, to "Wer hofft in Gott und dem vertraut". There it has the accompaniment of *Corno di caccia*, *Oboi I & II*, Strings, and *Continuo*, with a very elaborate bass part, and with interludes.

The instrumentation for the present use of the

chorale is as follows: soprano, *Flauti I & II* and *Viole I & II;* alto, *Viola III;* tenor, *Viola IV;* and bass, *Fagotto* and *Continuo* (unfigured).

Bach wrote two preludes on this melody: one in the *Orgelbüchlein,* and the other a fugue in the miscellaneous preludes.

The English translation of this stanza was made by J. C. Jacobi, and appeared in 1722.

41. Ein' feste Burg ist unser Gott

Though this melody is generally attributed to Martin Luther, there has been much discussion of the extent to which it is borrowed from earlier sources, in accordance with a custom common in the early days of chorale melodies. In this form, save for two notes which were doubtless printer's errors, it appeared with this hymn in Jobst Gutknecht's *Kirche Gesenge* (Nürnberg: 1531) and in Joseph Klug's *Geistliche Lieder zu Wittemberg* (Wittenberg: 1535).

Other Bach harmonizations of this melody are No. 20 in the Edition of 1784 and No. 250 in the Edition of 1786.

The instrumentation for Cantata 80 calls for *Trombe I, II, & III, Timpani, Oboi I & II, Oboi d'amore I & II, Taille, Oboe da caccia, Violini I & II,* and *Viola,* with a special part, in addition to the *Continuo,* for *Violoncello* or *Violone ed Organo.* This instrumentation was probably used in full for the accompaniment of the chorale.

Although this collection has not attempted to include in its references the great list of fantasias which are built upon chorale melodies, a few such examples are so compelling as to call for special mention. Among these is Cantata No. 80, "Ein' feste Burg". The opening chorus is one of the outstanding choral compositions of all time. The chorale in this composition is used in two ways: first, each verse-line is made the basis of a fugal exposition, and then the whole composition is encased within a canon of the octave, presenting the complete chorale melody between the high Trumpet above and the Organ and Bassoon below. In the second movement, a duet for soprano and bass, the soprano sings the chorale melody in slightly ornate form, accompanied by the Oboe, which presents the melody with greater ornamentation than the soprano. The fifth movement of the Cantata is a unison chorale, with a descriptive orchestral part of great dramatic intensity; this chorale stands as an affirmation of Faith in the strife against the forces of Wickedness. The final movement is the chorale, simply stated.

Schweitzer is inclined to think that Bach composed his prelude on this melody for the opening of the organ at Mühlhausen in 1709. See Spitta (I, 395) for the indication of the registration.

This is Luther's most famous hymn; for an account of it, see Julian's *Dictionary,* p. 322. There, eighteen English translations in common use are listed, and thirty-one less familiar ones. A famous version is that made by Thomas Carlyle in his only notable venture into hymnody, for his essay on "Luther's Psalm" in *Fraser's Magazine,* 1831. The translation used here is that of Catherine Winkworth, in the *Chorale Book for England* (1863).

42. Erhalt' uns, Herr, bei deinem Wort

This melody and hymn were first published in Joseph Klug's *Geistliche Lieder zu Wittemberg* (Wittenberg: 1543). In the original melody as it appears in books of 1593 and later, a sharp is prefixed to the fourth note (the sixth in Bach's version).

This is apparently the only chorale harmonization of this melody by J. S. Bach.

The instrumentation is as follows: soprano, *Violino I* and *Oboi I & II;* alto, *Violino II* and *Oboe da caccia;* tenor, *Viola;* and bass, *Continuo.*

Luther's hymn "Erhalt' uns, Herr, bei deinem Wort" was probably written in 1541, for a service of prayer to be held against the Turks. (Even in England in 1565 there was a prayer "for the delivery of those Christians that are now invaded by the Turk".) The translation given here is from the *Moravian Hymn Book* (1754).

43. Ermuntre dich, mein schwacher Geist

This hymn and tune were first published in Johann Schop's *Himlischer Lieder* (Lüneburg: 1641). The melody is by Schop.

Bach used this melody for other harmonizations: in Cantata 11, to the words "Nun liegt alles unter dir", and in Cantata 43 to "Du Lebensfürst, Herr Jesu Christ" and "Zieh' uns dir nach, so laufen wir".

The instrumentation he has given for the present use is as follows: soprano, *Flauti traversi I & II, Oboi d'amore I & II,* and *Violino I;* alto, *Oboe da caccia I* and *Violino II;* tenor, *Oboe da caccia II* and *Viola;* and bass, *Organo e Continuo.*

The hymn is by Johann Rist (1607-1667), one of the most popular of German hymn-writers. It is a Christmas hymn of twelve long stanzas, based on Isaiah 9:2-7. This English translation of the ninth stanza was made by Albert Riemenschneider for this edition.

44. Es ist das Heil uns kommen her

This melody was published with this hymn in the *Etlich Christlich lider* (Wittenberg: 1524) and also in other books of the same year. Zahn says the melody belonged to the Easter song "Freu dich, du werte Christenheit", and that it was known in the fifteenth century.

Other Bach harmonizations of this melody are in the Wedding-chorale "Sei Lob und Ehr' dem höchsten Gut" (No. 115 of the present edition), in Cantata 86 to "Die Hoffnung wart't der rechten Zeit", in Cantata 117 to "Ich rief dem Herrn in meiner Noth" and "So kommet vor sein Angesicht", and in Cantata 155 to "Ob sich's anliess', als wollt' er nicht".

The instrumentation for this chorale in Cantata 9 is as follows: soprano, *Flauto traverso* (in *8va*), *Oboe d'amore*, and *Violino I;* alto, *Violino II;* tenor, *Viola;* and bass, *Continuo.*

Schweitzer calls attention to "the motive of joy", a rhythm of an eighth-note followed by two sixteenth-notes, in a prelude in the *Orgelbüchlein.*

Paulus Speratus (1484-1551) was associated with Luther in preparing the first Lutheran hymn book, and wrote three of the eight hymns it contained. One of these is "Es ist das Heil uns kommen her", probably written in 1523. The English translation (1725) is by J. C. Jacobi.

45. Es ist genug: Herr, wenn es dir gefällt

This melody is by Johann Rudolph Ahle, and was published in his *Neuer Geistlicher Arien* (Mühlhausen: 1662) to this hymn.

This seems to be the only harmonization by Bach of this chorale.

The instrumentation for this setting is as follows: soprano, *Corno, Oboe d'amore I,* and *Violino I;* alto, *Oboe d'amore II* and *Violino II;* tenor, *Viola;* and bass, *Continuo* (unfigured).

The hymn is by Franz Joachim Burmeister (born at Lüneburg, died there in 1672). It has never come into common English use. The translation was made by Charles N. Boyd for this edition.

46. Gott des Himmels und der Erden

In this instance, hymn and tune are by the same person. Heinrich Albert's words appeared with his melody in Part V of his *Arien oder Melodeyen* (Königsberg: 1642). A revised form appeared in the Darmstadt *Cantional* of 1687.

No other Bach harmonization of this melody has yet been found.

The instrumentation given for this chorale in the "Christmas Oratorio" assigns *Oboi d'amore I & II* and *Violino I* to the soprano, *Violino II* to the alto, *Viola* to the tenor, and *Organo e Continuo* to the bass.

Heinrich Albert (1604-1651) was organist of the Königsberg Cathedral at the age of twenty-seven; later he became a member of the Poetical Union of Königsberg. His morning hymn "Gott des Himmels und der Erden" has been a favorite morning prayer in Germany. The translation is by Albert Riemenschneider.

47. Helft mir Gott's Güte preisen

A secular song "Ich ging einmal spazieren" was the source of two chorale melodies. One of these was set to "Von Gott will ich nicht lassen", by Ludwig Helmbold, in Joachim Magdeburg's *Christliche und Tröstliche Tischgesenge* (Erfurt: 1571). The other, in two forms, appeared with "Helft mir Gott's Güte preisen" in Wolfgang Figulus's *Weynacht-Liedlein* (Frankfurt an der Oder: 1575 [1569?]).

Bach harmonized the latter form of the melody in Cantata 28 to "All' solch' dein' Güt' wir preisen" and in Cantata 183 to "Du bist ein Geist, der lehret".

The *Orgelbüchlein* contains a prelude on this melody.

The instrumentation for this chorale is as follows: soprano, *Corno da caccia, Oboe I,* and *Violino I;* alto, *Oboe II, Violino II,* and *Viola;* tenor, not specified; and bass, *Continuo* (unfigured).

This hymn for the New Year, "Helft mir Gott's Güte preisen", was written by Paul Eber (1511-1569), teacher, preacher, and hymn-writer at Wittenberg. The English translation of this stanza was made by J. C. Jacobi, and was published in 1722.

48. Herr Gott, dich loben wir

Zahn believes that this melody was used with Luther's translation of the "Te Deum laudamus" in the non-extant first edition (1529) of Joseph Klug's *Geistliche Lieder*, for it was in the second edition (Wittenberg: 1535). In a later edition (1543) it was arranged for antiphonal singing. The melody is a simplified version of the old plainsong melody.

The complete melody appears as No. 205 in the Edition of 1786. Bach uses various divisions of this complete form in his vocal works. A small section of the melody is used as the basis of the opening chorus in Cantata 16. In Cantata 190 he uses the two opening clauses in harmonized form with alternating recitatives. In Cantata 119 he employs a section as the concluding chorale, the melody of which agrees with the latter half of the present harmonization, which is from Cantata 120.

No instrumentation is indicated for this chorale. The cantata is scored for *Oboi d'amore I & II, Trombe I, II, & III, Timpani, Violino concertante,* and the usual Strings. The *Continuo* of the chorale was not figured.

Schweitzer does not consider that the organ piece printed under this name ought to be included in the collections of Bach's chorale-preludes; he thinks it a long example of Bach's mature style of an accompaniment, rather than an organ solo. It resembles No. 205 of the Edition of 1786.

The translation was made by Albert Riemenschneider for this edition.

49. HERR JESU CHRIST, DU HÖCHSTES GUT

This chorale melody is derived from a rather unusual source. A hymn "Wenn mein Stündlein vorhanden ist" was published with a four-part setting in *Harmoniae hymnorum scholae Gorlicensis* (1599). From the tenor of this setting was developed the present melody, which came into common use with the hymn "Herr Jesu Christ, du höchstes Gut", after its first appearance in the Dresden *Gesangbuch* of 1593.

Other harmonizations by Bach of this melody are found in two other cantatas: No. 113, to "Stärk' mich mit deinem Freudengeist" and to "Herr Jesu Christ, du höchstes Gut" (the latter with *Oboi I & II*, Strings, *Continuo obbligato,* and interludes) ; and No. 168 to "Stärk mich mit deinem Freudengeist". It is also No. 73 in the Edition of 1784.

The instrumentation here specified is as follows: soprano, *Tromba, Oboi I & II,* and *Violino I;* alto, *Violino II;* tenor, *Viola;* and bass, *Continuo.*

The text is the twelfth stanza of a hymn "Herr Jesu Christ, ich schrei zu dir", by an anonymous author, published in Christopher Demantius's *Threnodiae* (Freiberg: 1620). The English translation was made by Charles N. Boyd for this edition.

50. HERR JESU CHRIST, WAHR'R MENSCH UND GOTT

Ambrosius Lobwasser (1515-1585) was an important factor in the connection of the Genevan Psalter with the Lutheran Church. His literal translations of the French versions, set to their original melodies, were published as *Der Psalter dess Königlichen Propheten Dauids, in deutsche reymen verstendiglich und deutlich gebracht* (Leipzig: 1573). In this book the French version of Psalm 127, "On a beau sa maison bastir", became "Wenn einer schon ein Haus aufbaut", with this melody, doubtless by Louis Bourgeois. The melody was adopted, with variants, for "Herr Jesu Christ, wahr'r Mensch und Gott", in Lutheran books.

Another Bach harmonization of a melody designated under the same title is No. 189 in the Edition of 1785.

The instrumentation for the chorale in Cantata 127 is as follows: soprano, *Flauti I & II* (*in 8va*) ; *Oboi I & II,* and *Violino I;* alto, *Violino II;* tenor, *Viola;* and bass, *Continuo* (unfigured) .

The hymn, "Herr Jesu Christ, wahr'r Mensch und Gott", was written by Paul Eber, perhaps before 1550. It is found in the Hamburg *Enchiridion* (1565), where it is entitled "A prayer to Christ for a happy departure from this troublous life". The text of this chorale is the eighth stanza of Eber's hymn. The English translation is by Dr. Emanuel Cronenwett (1841-1931), for many years a Lutheran pastor in Ohio and Pennsylvania, widely known for his translations of German hymns. This version was made in 1878.

51. HERR, WIE DU WILL'T, SO SCHICK'S MIT MIR

This melody is in the *Ordnung des Herren Nachtmahl* (Strassburg: 1525) and in the Strassburg *Kirchenamt* of the same year, in both books to the hymn "Aus tiefer Noth schrei ich zu dir". With somewhat altered rhythms the melody became popular as a setting for other hymns, especially "Herr, wie du will't, so schick's mit mir".

Other harmonizations by Bach of this melody are No. 144 in the Edition of 1785 and No. 317 in the Edition of 1787.

The instrumentation indicated for the present use is as follows: soprano, *Oboe* and *Violino I;* alto, *Violino II;* tenor, *Viola;* and bass, *Continuo* (unfigured) .

In Caspar Bienemann's *Betbüchlein* (Leipzig: 1582), his hymn "Herr, wie du will't, so schick's mit mir" appears for the first time in print, having been written in 1574. For an account of it, see Julian's *Dictionary*, p. 142. The English translation was made by Dr. Emanuel Cronenwett in 1877.

52. ICH FREUE MICH IN DIR

This melody is found set to "O stilles Gotteslamm" in Johann Balthasar König's *Harmonischer Lieder-Schatz*, a large collection published in 1738. Zahn states that Bach knew the melody as early as 1733. The claim that Bach himself may have composed it is discussed in C. S. Terry's *Bach's Chorals*, Part II, p. 393. Terry concludes that the balance of probability is against Bach's being the composer of the tune.

The instrumentation specified for this chorale in Cantata 133 is as follows: soprano, *Cornetto, Oboe d'amore I*, and *Violino I*; alto, *Oboe d'amore II* and *Violino II*; tenor, *Viola*; and bass, *Continuo*.

Caspar Ziegler's Christmas hymn "Ich freue mich in dir" was published in the *Geistreiches Gesang Buch* (Halle: 1697). The English translation was made for this edition by Charles N. Boyd.

53. JESU, DER DU MEINE SEELE

This melody appeared in 1642 to a secular song by Johann Rist, "Daphnis ging für wenig Tagen", and the next year to "Ferdinand, du grosser Kaiser". Twenty years later, in M. Nicolaus Stenger's *Christlich-Neu-vermehrt und gebessertes Gesangbuch* (Erfurt: 1663), the melody is set to Rist's hymn "Jesu, der du meine Seele".

Other harmonizations by Bach of this melody are in the following: Cantata 105, to "Nun ich weiss, du wirst mir stillen", with three obbligato instrumental voices; the Edition of 1784 as No. 37; the Edition of 1786 as No. 269; and the Edition of 1787 as No. 368.

The score indicates the following instrumentation for this setting: soprano, *Flauto traverso* (*in 8va*), *Oboe I, Corno*, and *Violino I*; alto, *Oboe II* and *Violino II*; tenor, *Viola*; and bass, *Continuo*.

Rist's Lenten hymn was first published in *Das erste Zehn* of his *Himlischer Lieder* (1641). The English translation has been made by Charles N. Boyd for this edition.

54. KOMMT HER ZU MIR, SPRICHT GOTTES SOHN

This melody has always been associated with this hymn. They appeared together on a broadsheet of 1530, entitled "Ain schöns newes Christlichs lyed".

Another Bach harmonization of this melody is found in Cantata 108, to the words "Dein Geist, den Gott vom Himmel giebt".

The instrumentation given here is as follows: soprano, *Tromba I, Oboe I*, and *Violino I*; alto, *Oboe II* and *Violino II*; tenor, *Oboe da caccia* and *Viola*; and bass, *Continuo*.

The stanza used in Cantata 74 is from a hymn by Paul Gerhardt, "Gott Vater, sende deinen Geist", and was first published in the Berlin edition of Crüger's *Praxis Pietatis Melica* (1653). The English translation was made by Charles N. Boyd for this edition.

55. MIT FRIED' UND FREUD' ICH FAHR' DAHIN

This melody and hymn were published together in Johann Walther's *Geystliche gesangk Buchleyn* (Wittenberg: 1524). Terry considers Luther the probable author of the tune.

Other Bach harmonizations of this melody are in

Cantata 95 (No. 109 in Book II of this edition), to "Mit Fried' und Freud' ich fahr' dahin", and in Cantata 125, to "Er ist das Heil und sel'ge Licht". It is also No. 49 in the Edition of 1784.

The instrumentation specified for the chorale in Cantata 83 is as follows: soprano, *Oboe I, Corno*, and *Violino I*; alto, *Oboe II* and *Violino II*; tenor, *Viola*; and bass, *Continuo*.

This melody is used for one of the preludes in the *Orgelbüchlein*. To Schweitzer it "depicts a joyous longing for death".

The hymn "Mit Fried' und Freud' ich fahr' dahin" is Luther's free rendering of the "Nunc Dimittis", the Song of Simeon, St. Luke 2:29-32. The English translation, by Catherine Winkworth, was made for her *Christian Singers of Germany* (1869).

56. NUN LASST UNS GOTT DEM HERREN

This hymn by Ludwig Helmbold was published with a four-part setting in his *Geistliche Lieder, den Gottseligen Christen zugericht* (Mühlhausen: 1575). Zahn suggests that the tenor of that setting should be regarded as the chief melody, in view of the monotonous soprano. Neither tenor nor soprano is very close to the present chorale melody. Other versions of the melody subsequently appeared, such as Nicolaus Selnecker's (1587) and Johann Crüger's (in *Praxis Pietatis Melica*, 1649).

Bach harmonized this melody in Cantata 79 to "Erhalt' uns in der Wahrheit" (with obbligato parts consisting of *Corni I & II* and *Timpani*) and in Cantata 194 to "Sprich Ja zu meinen Thaten" and "Mit Segen mich beschütte".

The instrumentation for the chorale in Cantata 165 is as follows: soprano, *Violino I*; alto, *Violino II*; tenor, *Viola*; and bass, *Fagotto* and *Continuo* (unfigured).

The translation is adapted from a quaint version in *The Supplement to German Psalmody* (1765).

57. NUN LOB', MEIN' SEEL', DEN HERREN

This hymn and tune were first published together in Johann Kugelmann's *News Gesanng, mit Dreyen stymmen* (Augsburg: 1540). The melody is probably by Kugelmann; as usual, it had developed many variants by Bach's time.

Bach's settings of the melody, in addition to the present example, occur in Cantata 29 to the words "Sei Lob und Preis" (see No. 111 of this edition), and in Cantata 167 to the same words, accompanied by *Clarino, Oboe*, Strings, and *Continuo obbligato*, with interludes. It is also No. 268 in the Edition of 1786, and No. 295 in the Edition of 1787.

The instrumentation specified by Bach for this use is as follows: soprano, *Oboi I & II* and *Violino I;* alto, *Violino II;* tenor, *Viola;* and bass, *Continuo* (unfigured).

The hymn, based on Psalm 103, is the only surviving hymn by Johann Graumann (1487-1541). It appeared on a broadsheet printed at Nürnberg in 1540. The English translation of this stanza was made by Catherine Winkworth for the *Chorale Book for England* (1863).

58. O GOTT, DU FROMMER GOTT

This melody, by an unknown composer, appeared in Ahashuerus Fritsch's *Himmels-Lust und Welt-Unlust* (Jena: 1679), with a hymn by J. J. Schütz, "Die Wollust dieser Welt". A new version of the melody, still with the Schütz hymn, appeared in the *Geistreiches Gesang-Buch* (Darmstadt: 1698), and a version of this tune became common in Saxony to the hymn "O Gott, du frommer Gott".

Bach made rather frequent use of this melody. In Cantata 64 and in Cantata 94 it is set to "Was frag' ich nach der Welt"; in Cantata 128, to "Alsdann so wirst du mich" (with *Corni I & II, obbligati*); in Cantata 129, to "Dem wir das Heilig itzt", accompanied by Strings, Woodwind, and Brass, with interludes. It is also No. 314 in the Edition of 1787.

The instrumentation for the present use is as follows: soprano, *Flauti traversi I & II, Oboi I & II,* and *Violino I;* alto, *Violino II;* tenor, *Viola;* and bass, *Continuo* (unfigured).

Johann Heermann's "O Gott, du frommer Gott" was one of 49 hymns in his *Devoti Musica Cordis* (Leipzig: 1630), there entitled "A Daily Prayer". The English translation is by Catherine Winkworth, in her *Lyra Germanica* (1858).

59. O HERRE GOTT, DEIN GÖTTLICH WORT

This hymn and tune were published in the 1527 edition of the Erfurt *Enchiridion,* signed A. H. Z. W., and became very popular during the Reformation. The initials are assumed to be those of Anark Herr zu Wildenfels.

Another harmonization of this tune by Bach is found in the Edition of 1784, No. 14.

The instrumentation for the chorale in Cantata 184 is as follows: soprano, *Flauti traversi I & II* and *Violino I;* alto, *Violino II;* tenor, *Viola;* and bass, *Continuo* (unfigured).

The English translation is from the *Moravian Hymn Book* (1754).

60. O WELT, ICH MUSS DICH LASSEN
(NUN RUHEN ALLE WÄLDER)

Early in the sixteenth century a secular song, the melody of which was attributed to Heinrich Isaak, became very popular. It was "Innsbruck, ich muss dich lassen", and was published in Georg Forster's *Ein ausszug guter alter und newer Teutscher liedlein* (Nürnberg: 1539). Johann Hesse's hymn for the dying, "O Welt, ich muss dich lassen", which appeared on a broadsheet printed at Nürnberg in 1555, is a transcription of this journeyman's-song; but apparently it was not printed with this tune before the *Gesangbuch, Darinnen Psalmen und Geistliche Lieder* (Eisleben: 1598). The word "Innsbruck" has persisted in the title, as frequently found with this melody in English and American hymnals.

Bach made several harmonizations of this popular melody. In addition to the present setting in the "St. Matthew Passion", he also used it in the same work to the words "Ich bin's, ich sollte büssen". In the "St. John Passion" it is also set to two stanzas, "Wer hat dich so geschlagen" and "Ich, ich und meine Sünden". In Cantatas 13 and 44 it is set to "So sei nun, Seele, deine", and in Cantata 97 to the same words, with Strings *obbligati* (this latter form is found as No. 113 in the present collection). Another setting is No. 288 in the Edition of 1787. Finally, it appears three times to "O Welt, sieh hier dein Leben" in the following editions: No. 275 in the Edition of 1786, No. 362 in the Edition of 1787, and No. 365 in the Edition of 1787.

The instrumentation for this setting assigns *Flauti traversi I & II, Oboi I & II,* and *Violino I* to the soprano; *Violino II* to the alto; *Viola* to the tenor; and *Organo e Continuo* to the bass. The translation is by John S. Dwight.

61. SCHWING' DICH AUF ZU DEINEM GOTT

Many melodies have been used for Paul Gerhardt's hymn "Schwing' dich auf zu deinem Gott". One of them was published in Daniel Vetter's *Musicalische Kirch- und Hauss-Ergötzlichkeit* (Leipzig: 1713), with Heinrich Albert's hymn "Einen guten Kampf hab' ich". A revision of this melody is in *Johann Sebastian Bachs vierstimmige Choralgesänge gesammlet von C. P. E. Bach* (1769).

This appears to be the only harmonization of this melody in Bach's works.

The instrumentation in this instance is as follows: soprano, *Corno I, Oboe I,* and *Violino I;* alto, *Oboe II* and *Violino II;* tenor, *Viola;* and bass, *Continuo.* The stanza here set is the second one in the Gerhardt hymn, which was first published in Crüger's *Praxis Pietatis Melica* (Berlin: 1653).

The translation was made by Albert Riemenschneider for this edition.

62. STRAF MICH NICHT IN DEINEM ZORN

This melody was published in the *Hundert ahnmuthig- und sonderbar geistlicher Arien* (Dresden: 1694), with the hymn by J. G. Albinus, "Straf mich nicht in deinem Zorn"; and from this first association, that title of the tune still persists. By 1710 the melody was set to the Freystein hymn used here.

This is the only harmonization by Bach of this tune.

The instrumentation for this setting in Cantata 115 is as follows: soprano, *Corno, Flauto, Oboe d'amore,* and *Violino I;* alto, *Violino II;* tenor, *Viola;* and bass, *Continuo.*

"Mache dich, mein Geist, bereit", Johann Burchard Freystein's hymn on the theme of watchfulness, was first printed in the *Geistreiches Gesang-Buch* (Halle: 1698). The stanza here used is the tenth and last. The English translation was made by Dr. Emanuel Cronenwett in 1878.

63. VATER UNSER IM HIMMELREICH

This melody, set to Luther's versification of "The Lord's Prayer", has been popular in Germany since its first appearance with these words in Valentin Schumann's *Geistliche lieder auffs new gebessert* (Leipzig: 1539). Some credit the melody to Luther himself, but without definite authority. The facsimile of Luther's draft of this hymn is reproduced in Winterfeld's *Dr. Martin Luthers deutsche Geistliche Lieder* (Leipzig: 1840). After the words, Luther drew a staff and wrote a melody on it, but crossed it out, apparently considering it unsuitable.

Bach made several other harmonizations of this melody. In the original version of the "St. John Passion" it is set to "Dein Will' gescheh', Herr Gott" with a different harmonization than that of the present one. It is found as No. 47 in the Edition of 1784. In Cantatas 90 and 101 it is set to "Leit' uns mit deiner rechten Hand"; and in Cantata 102 it is set to "Heut' lebst du, heut' bekehre dich" and to "Hilf, o Herr Jesu, hilf du mir". It is No. 291 in the Edition of 1787.

The instrumentation for the present use is as follows: soprano, *Flauti traversi I & II, Oboi I & II,* and *Violino I;* alto, *Violino II;* tenor, *Viola;* and bass, *Organo e Continuo.*

One setting of the melody is found in the *Orgelbüchlein;* and three others, including one long canon, occur among the other chorale-preludes.

This hymn has been regarded by some as Luther's finest. Each of the first eight stanzas expounds one of the phrases of the Lord's Prayer, and the ninth stanza is on the *Amen.* The English translation of the fourth stanza was made by Catherine Winkworth in the *Chorale Book for England* (1863).

64. VON GOTT WILL ICH NICHT LASSEN

The sources from which this melody is derived are given in the note on No. 47 of this book. The melody is known either as "Von Gott will ich nicht lassen" or "Helft mir Gott's Güte preisen", according to its use.

Another Bach harmonization of this melody is in Cantata 11, to the words "Wann soll es doch geschehen", extended and with interludes, with accompaniment of *Trombe I, II, & III, Timpani, Flauti traversi I & II, Oboi I & II,* Strings, and *Continuo.* In Cantata 107 are two settings: one, which is very elaborate, to "Was willst du dich betrüben", with *Flauti traversi I & II, Oboi d'amore I & II,* Strings, and Organ and *Continuo;* and one also with interludes to "Herr, gieb, dass ich dein' Ehre", with three obbligato instrumental parts, Organ, and *Continuo.* In both of these the soprano part is duplicated by the *Corno da caccia.* In the unfinished cantata "Lobt ihn mit Herz und Munde", Bach has set the melody to the hymn which furnishes the title of the cantata; here it has undergone some change in form. It is No. 114 in the Edition of 1785, and Nos. 331 and 363 in the Edition of 1787.

In the chorale-prelude on this melody, the *cantus firmus* is in the pedal. The style of the piece reminds Schweitzer of Buxtehude.

The instruments specified for the chorale in Cantata 73 are as follows: soprano, *Corno, Oboe I,* and *Violino I;* alto, *Oboe II* and *Violino II;* tenor, *Viola;* and bass, *Continuo.*

The story of Ludwig Helmbold's hymn of trust, "Von Gott will ich nicht lassen", is given in Julian's *Dictionary.* Its first publication seems to have been on a broadsheet in 1563 or 1564. The English translation is from the *Moravian Hymn Book,* 1754.

65. WACHET AUF, RUFT UNS DIE STIMME

Philip Nicolai's hymn "Wachet auf, ruft uns die Stimme", was published with this melody in his *Frewden Spiegel dess ewigen Lebens* (Frankfurt am Main: 1599). Nicolai is usually credited with being the composer, or perhaps the compiler, of the melody. Both hymn and tune are of first rank.

This seems to be the only Bach harmonization of this melody.

The indicated instrumentation is as follows: soprano, *Violino piccolo* (*in 8va*), *Corno, Oboe I*, and *Violino I*; alto, *Oboe II* and *Violino II*; tenor, *Taille* and *Viola*; and bass, *Continuo*.

The chorale-prelude for organ, one of the six "Schübler Chorales", is taken from the setting in this cantata.

The English translation was made by Dr. Emanuel Cronenwett in 1879.

66. Warum betrübst du dich, mein Herz

This hymn and tune are found in a manuscript of Monoetius, dated Crailsheim, 1565. Both hymn and tune may be older; the hymn has been ascribed to Hans Sachs (1494-1576). Zahn remarks on the early and wide popularity of the melody.

Bach set this melody to "Weil du mein Gott und Vater bist" in Cantata 138, with accompaniment of *Oboi d'amore I & II*, Strings, and *Continuo*, with free interludes. It is No. 145 in the Edition of 1785 and No. 299 in the Edition of 1787.

The instrumentation indicated for the setting in Cantata 47 is as follows: soprano, *Oboi I & II* and *Violino I*; alto, *Violino II*; tenor, *Viola*; and bass, *Continuo*.

The translation is found in Catherine Winkworth's *Lyra Germanica* (1858).

67. Was mein Gott will, das g'scheh' allzeit

The original of this melody seems to be a secular song "Il me souffit de tous mas maulx", in Pierre Attaignant's *Trente et quatre chansons musicales,* printed at Paris between 1529 and 1534. In Germany it appeared with this hymn in Joachim Magdeburg's *Christliche und Tröstliche Tischgesenge* (Erfurt: 1572 [or 1571]).

Other Bach harmonizations of this melody are found in the following cantatas: No. 65, to "Ei nun, mein Gott, so fall' ich dir"; ·No. 92, to the same words, with recitative interludes; No. 92, to "Soll ich denn auch des Todes Weg"; No. 103, to "Ich hab' dich einen Augenblick"; No. 111, to "Noch eins, Herr, will ich bitten dich"; No. 144 (and the "St. Matthew Passion") to "Was mein Gott will, das g'scheh' allzeit".

The instrumentation specified for the use in Cantata 72 is as follows: soprano, *Oboi I & II* and *Violino I*; alto, *Violino II*; tenor, *Viola*; and bass, *Continuo*.

This hymn of trust, "Was mein Gott will, das g'scheh' allzeit", dates from 1554 or earlier, several versions of it appearing at different times. It is the only hymn ascribed to Albrecht, Margrave of Brandenburg-Culmbach in Lower Franconia (1522-1557).

The English translation was made for this edition by Charles N. Boyd.

68. Wir Christenleut'

This melody and hymn are found together in a manuscript, *Kurze Comedie von der Geburt Christi,* dated 1589. Their first appearance in print seems to have been in Martin Fritzsch's *Gesangbuch* (Dresden: 1593).

Other harmonizations by Bach of this melody occur as follows: in Cantata 110, to "Alleluja! Alleluja! gelobt sei Gott!"; in Cantata 142 to the same words, with Flutes, Oboes, Violins, Violas, and *Continuo*, with short interludes; and in the "Christmas Oratorio" to "Seid froh, dieweil, seid froh".

The instrumentation indicated in this setting is as follows: soprano, *Corno I, Oboe I*, and *Violino I*; alto, *Oboe II* and *Violino II*; tenor, *Viola*; and bass, *Continuo*.

Spitta says of a prelude on this melody in the *Orgelbüchlein* that it speaks of "firm belief in the Christmas tidings"; another organ-prelude on this theme is a trio with *cantus firmus* in the pedals.

Two Lutheran clergymen named Caspar Füger, father and son, lived in Dresden in the last years of the sixteenth century. Some think that the father was the author of the hymn and the son was the composer of the above melody. The English version is by Catherine Winkworth, in the *Chorale Book for England* (1863).

69. Allein zu dir, Herr Jesu Christ

This hymn and tune were published, apparently for the first time, on a broadsheet about 1541. A revised version of the melody appeared in Valentin Babst's *Geystliche Lieder* (Leipzig: 1545), and was promptly included in other collections.

Another Bach harmonization of this melody is No. 358 in the Edition of 1787.

The instrumentation for this chorale in Cantata 33 is as follows: soprano, *Oboe I* and *Violino I*; alto, *Oboe II* and *Violino II*; tenor, *Viola*; and bass, *Organo e Continuo*.

This is the fourth stanza of a hymn of penitence by Johannes Schneesing. The English translation is by Catherine Winkworth, originally published in her *Lyra Germanica* (1858) and later revised for the *Chorale Book for England*.

70. Christ, unser Herr, zum Jordan kam

This is the melody which was used in Johann Walther's *Geystliche gesangk Buchleyn* (Wittenberg:

1524) for Luther's hymn "Es wollt uns Gott genädig sein". Since 1543, in Joseph Klug's *Geistliche Lieder* (Wittenberg), it has been associated with Luther's baptismal hymn "Christ, unser Herr, zum Jordan kam".

Bach used this melody in Cantata 7, to the words "Das Aug' allein das Wasser sieht". It is also No. 65 in the Edition of 1784.

The instrumentation specified for the present use is as follows: soprano, *Oboe I* and *Violino I;* alto, *Oboe II* and *Violino II;* tenor, *Oboe da caccia* and *Viola;* and bass, *Continuo.*

Two preludes on this melody are found among the Bach organ works. See Schweitzer, II, p. 58, concerning these pieces.

The stanza here set by Bach is taken from Paul Gerhardt's "Was alle Weisheit in der Welt", which was first published in Crüger's *Praxis Pietatis Melica* (Berlin: 1653). The English translation, by Albert Riemenschneider, was made for this edition.

71. Christum wir sollen loben schon

Luther's translation of the Latin hymn appeared with a plainsong melody in *Psalmen und geystliche Lieder* (Strassburg: 1537). A version of the melody had already appeared in the Erfurt *Enchiridion* of 1524.

This is the only harmonization of this chorale by J. S. Bach.

The instruments specified for this chorale in Cantata 121 are as follows: soprano, *Cornetto, Oboe d'amore,* and *Violino I;* alto, *Trombone I* and *Violino II;* tenor, *Trombone II* and *Viola;* and bass, *Trombone III col Continuo.*

In his remarks on the setting of this melody in the *Orgelbüchlein,* Schweitzer says: "The simple arabesque that entwines the melody of the Christmas Chorale is consummately effective. It embraces a whole world of unutterable joy" (II, 67). The other prelude is a short fughetta.

The hymn is taken from an alphabetical poem on the life of Christ, "Paean Alphabeticus de Christo", written by Sedulius, who died about 450. Luther's German translation, "Christum wir sollen loben schon", was first published in the Erfurt *Enchiridion* of 1524 and in Johann Walther's *Geystliche gesangk Buchleyn* (Wittenberg: 1524). The English translation of the eighth stanza was made by Richard Massie in 1854.

72. Freu' dich sehr, o meine Seele

For the history of the melody used here, see No. 11 of this collection.

Bach made frequent use of this melody in his cantatas. In No. 19 it is set to the words "Lass dein' Engel mit mir fahren" (here with the accompaniment of three Trumpets, two Oboes, Taille, and Strings); in No. 25 to "Ich will alle meine Tage"; in Cantata 32 to "Mein Gott, öffne mir die Pforten" (No. 11 of this collection); in No. 39 to "Selig sind, die aus Erbarmen"; in No. 70 to "Freu' dich sehr, o meine Seele"; and in No. 194 to "Heiliger Geist in's Himmelsthrone". It is also found as No. 297 in the Edition of 1787.

The instrumentation given for the present use is as follows: soprano, *Flauti traversi I & II* (in 8va), *Oboi I & II,* and *Violino I;* alto, *Violino II;* tenor, *Viola;* and bass, *Organo e Continuo.*

The hymn from which this stanza is taken is by Johannes Olearius, and was first published in his *Geistliche Singe-Kunst* (Leipzig: 1671), to the melody used here. Like this Bach cantata, the hymn is for St. John Baptist's Day. The English translation was made by Catherine Winkworth for the *Chorale Book for England* (1863).

73. Freuet euch, ihr Christen

This melody, with Keymann's hymn, was published in Andreas Hammerschmidt's *Musicalischer Andachten Geistlicher Moteten undt Concerten* (Freiberg: 1646).

This is the only setting by Bach of this chorale.

The instruments specified for this chorale in Cantata 40 are as follows: soprano, *Corno I, Oboe I,* and *Violino I;* alto, *Oboe II* and *Violino II;* tenor, *Viola;* and bass, *Continuo* (unfigured).

Christian Keymann (1607-1662) is said to have written this hymn for his students to sing at Christmas, 1645. The English translation by Catherine Winkworth is from the *Chorale Book for England* (1863).

74. Herzlich lieb hab' ich dich, o Herr

The oldest known appearance of this melody is in Bernhard Schmid's *Zwey Bücher Einer Neuen Kunstlichen Tablatur auf Orgel und Instrument* (Strassburg: 1577). Zahn considered it as of still earlier, but as yet undiscovered, origin.

Other Bach harmonizations of this melody are as follows: in the "St. John Passion", where it is set to "Ach Herr, lass dein lieb' Engelein"; in Cantata 149, to the same words; and in the Edition of 1786 as No. 277.

The instrumentation of this chorale in Cantata 174 calls for the following: soprano, *Oboe I* and *Violino*

I & II; alto, *Oboe II* and *Violino III;* tenor, *Taille* and *Viole I, II, & III;* and bass, *Continuo.*

This hymn for the dying was written by Martin Schalling, pastor at Strassburg, apparently about 1567, and was published in *Kurtze und sonderliche Newe Symbola* (Nürnberg: 1571). The English translation is by Dr. Philip Schaff, in his *Christ in Song* (1869).

75. ICH DANK' DIR, LIEBER HERRE

This melody appeared originally in a secular song "Entlaubt ist uns der Walde", which was known as early as 1532. In Johann Horn's *Ein Gesangbuch der Brüder inn Behemen und Merherrn* (Nürnberg: 1544), it is set to his hymn "Lob Gott getrost mit Singen". In a simpler form it was assigned to "Ich dank' dir, lieber Herre", in *Praxis Pietatis Melica* (Frankfurt: 1662).

Two other harmonizations by Bach of this melody are found as No. 2 in the Edition of 1784 and as No. 272 in the Edition of 1786.

The instrumentation for this chorale in Cantata 37 is as follows: soprano, *Oboe d'amore I* and *Violino I;* alto, *Oboe d'amore II* and *Violino II;* tenor, *Viola;* and bass, *Continuo.*

Johann Kolross's morning hymn, of which the fourth stanza is here set by Bach, was first published separately at Nürnberg about 1535. The English translation was made by Charles N. Boyd for this edition.

76. IST GOTT MEIN SCHILD UND HELFERSMANN

Ernst Christoph Homburg's hymn "Ist Gott mein Schild und Helfersmann" was first published in his *Geistlicher Lieder* (Naumburg: 1658-59), but with a different melody. It was set to the present melody in *Hundert ahnmuthig- und sonderbahr geistlicher Arien* (Dresden: 1694).

This is the only known Bach harmonization of this melody.

The instrumentation for the chorale is as follows: soprano, *Oboi I & II* and *Violino I;* alto, *Violino II;* tenor, *Viola;* and bass, *Continuo* (unfigured).

The translation of this stanza from Homburg's hymn has been made by Charles N. Boyd for this edition.

77-81. JESU, MEINE FREUDE

It is a difficult matter to isolate any Bach composition as the one outstanding example of his genius and resourcefulness — so many of his compositions could be cited for such a description. Yet, in some ways, the motet "Jesu, meine Freude" deserves special consideration. The motet, in the Leipzig churches where Bach directed the music, came after the organ prelude for the early service and vespers, and was omitted only in Lent, when the organ was not used. Apparently the concern of Bach and his predecessors was for the cantata and not for the motet; they simply used traditional settings for a routine part of the service. Only six motets can now be definitely ascribed to Bach, and three of these are known to have been composed for special occasions. Schweitzer says that "Jesu, meine Freude" was composed in 1723 for the funeral of a Frau Käse. The six stanzas of Johann Franck's hymn, and Romans 8: 1, 2, 9, 10, and 11, form the text of this motet.

The first stanza is set for four voices, in what Bach would call *simplici stilo*. Then comes a strongly contrasting five-part chorus, in $\frac{2}{3}$ measure, on the first of the verses from Romans: "There is therefore now no condemnation to them which are in Christ Jesus, who walk not after the flesh, but after the Spirit". This is followed by the second stanza of the hymn, also set for five voices. The storm of the world is musically suggested by the motion of the lower voices. A trio for two sopranos and alto now takes up the second Biblical verse: "For the law of the Spirit of life in Christ Jesus hath made me free from the law of sin and death".

The third stanza, the music of which is omitted in this edition, is seldom found in the English translations of the hymn. As given by J. C. Jacobi in 1722 it is:

> I defy all evil,
> Sword, death, hell, and devil,
>   With their slavish fear;
> Tho' the world's me stinging,
> Yet will I be singing,
>   For my God is near.
> Satan's clan may curse and ban;
> Earth and hell, howe'er they riot,
>   Yet must soon be quiet.

For this stanza Bach forsakes the direct statement of the chorale melody, and presents a new, elaborated version in $\frac{3}{4}$ measure in chorale-fantasia form. The sentiment of the text is that of the music. Schweitzer has remarked that "the devil appeals strongly to the musician in Bach". Taking the Old Testament typification of Satan by the serpent, Bach is apt to suggest him by curving patterns such as characterize the first part of this highly descriptive chorus.

Then comes a fugue to the Biblical verse: "But ye are not in the flesh, but in the Spirit, if so be that the Spirit of God dwell in you"; followed by the closing part of this highly impressive middle section of the motet: "Now if any man have not the Spirit of Christ, he is none of his".

The first and second sopranos are united on the chorale melody for the next stanza of the hymn, but the lower voices utter contempt for earthly treasure and honor. The next episode is a trio for alto, tenor, and bass, to the Scriptural verse: "And if Christ be in you, the body is dead because of sin; but the Spirit is life because of righteousness". Then the basses are silent, and the two sopranos and the tenor gently begin the renunciation expressed by the words of the next stanza. At the ninth measure the alto takes up the chorale melody as a *cantus firmus*. After this long stanza the material of the second chorus now returns in new form, with the words of the last verse from Romans: "But if the Spirit of him that raised up Jesus from the dead dwell in you, he that raised up Christ from the dead shall also quicken your mortal bodies by his Spirit that dwelleth in you". The motet closes with the last stanza of the hymn, set in the same way as the first.

This long explanation is perhaps warranted in order to explain the setting of these five chorale treatments, and to lead to a better comprehension of Bach's achievements in this motet. Spitta said, "The germ of Protestant Christianity is embodied in this great work"; and Schweitzer felt that the text could be regarded as Bach's sermon upon life and death. Musically, the work is remarkable for its form as well as its content. Bound together by the chorale melody in its repeated appearances, and by the use of the same material for the second and next-to-last choruses, and the restatement of the first chorale at the close, the added sections supply contrast of the most valuable sort. From the gentle beginning, Bach proceeds steadily to the stirring climax of the middle section, and as steadily to the serene confidence of the last stanza. To modern ears the use of the key of E minor for eight of the eleven movements may appear unusual, but it was not so regarded in Bach's day. The fugue is in G major, the second trio in C major, and the section where the alto has the chorale melody is in A minor. The alternation of three-part, four-part, and five-part writing is noteworthy. Though the $\frac{4}{4}$ measure of the chorale seems to predominate, the second principal chorus and its reappearance are in $\frac{3}{2}$ measure, two movements are in $\frac{3}{4}$, one in $\frac{12}{8}$, and one in $\frac{2}{4}$ measure. Thus a noble text, one which evidently set forth Bach's personal convictions, is wedded to music which not only illustrates it perfectly but also, on its own account, is a notable and perfect musical structure.

Probably composed in 1723, the score was not printed until 1803, and then with unfortunate textual changes by J. G. Schicht, who was Cantor of the Thomasschule from 1810-1823. Vol. 39 of the Bachgesellschaft Edition, in which the motets are edited by Franz Wüllner, was not published until 1889.

The melody by Johann Crüger first appeared with this hymn in *Praxis Pietatis Melica* (Berlin: 1653). In addition to the harmonizations in this motet, Bach has harmonized the melody in the following cantatas: No. 64, to "Gute Nacht, o Wesen"; No. 81, to "Unter deinen Schirmen"; and No. 87, to "Muss ich sein betrübet?" It is also No. 355 in the Edition of 1787.

It was customary to use the Cembalo or Organ to accompany the motets during Bach's time. It is also affirmed that various instruments were used to duplicate the voices for performances out-of-doors, but no instruments are indicated for this score.

Bach wrote two organ pieces on this melody: the fantasia (Peters VI, 29), which is evidently a youthful work, and the prelude in the *Orgelbüchlein*. Schweitzer says of the rhythm in the lower voices of the latter that it expresses mystic adoration.

The hymn is by Johann Franck (1618-1677), lawyer, burgomaster, and deputy to the *Landtag*. He was known for his secular poetry, but his hymns have been much more highly appreciated. "Jesu, meine Freude" appeared in *Andachts Zymbeln* (Freyberg: 1655) and was soon widely used. Peter the Great directed its translation into Russian in 1724.

The English translation was made by Catherine Winkworth, in the *Chorale Book for England* (1863). The verbal changes necessary in the adaptation of these settings are as found in the Schirmer vocal score of this motet.

82. KOMM, JESU, KOMM

This melody is doubtless by J. S. Bach, and is not found elsewhere than in the present instance. The words are from an anonymous hymn, published in Paul Wagner's *Andächtiger Seelen geistliches Brandund Gantz-Opfer* (Leipzig: 1697). In his *Bach's Chorals*, II, 490, Charles Sanford Terry speculates on the possible author of the hymn.

This is the only harmonization by Bach of this melody.

No instrumentation was indicated for the chorale in the score of the motet in which it occurs, *Komm, Jesu, komm*. In Bach's time the motet was usually accompanied by Organ or Cembalo.

The English translation was made for this edition by Albert Riemenschneider.

83. LIEBSTER GOTT, WANN WERD' ICH STERBEN?

Caspar Neumann (1648-1715) was an outstanding preacher and a popular hymn-writer. Most of his hymns appeared, signed with his initials, in *Vollständige Kirchen- und Haus-Music*, about 1700. The melody was written for this hymn by Daniel Vetter for Cantor Jakob Wilisius, at whose funeral in 1695 it was sung. The first publication of the hymn and tune together was in Vetter's *Musicalische Kirch- und Hauss-Ergötzlichkeit*, Part II (Leipzig: 1713).

This is the only harmonization by Bach of this melody.

The instrumentation specified for this chorale is as follows: soprano, *Violino I, Flauto traverso (in 8va), Oboe d'amore I,* and *Corno;* alto, *Violino II* and *Oboe d'amore II;* tenor, *Viola;* and bass, *Continuo.*

The translation is by Albert Riemenschneider.

84. NUN BITTEN WIR DEN HEILIGEN GEIST

The five-line stanza "Nun bitten wir den heiligen Geist" dates back to the thirteenth century, and was one of the few vernacular hymns used in church before the Reformation. To this ancient stanza Luther added three more, first published in Johann Walther's *Geystliche gesangk Buchleyn* (Wittenberg: 1524). The melody may have been taken by Walther from an earlier version.

Other Bach harmonizations of this melody are in Cantata 169, to "Du süsse Liebe, schenk' uns deine Gunst", and in the Edition of 1784, as No. 36.

In this Wedding Cantata the instrumentation is for *Trombe I, II, & III, Timpani, Oboi I & II, Oboi d'amore I & II, Fagotto,* Strings, and *Continuo.* No instrumentation is indicated for the chorale in the score, and the *Continuo* is not figured.

The English translation is by an anonymous writer in *Some Other Hymns and Poems* (London: 1752).

85. NUN FREUT EUCH, LIEBEN CHRISTEN G'MEIN

Luther's first congregational hymn was "Nun freut euch, lieben Christen g'mein", written in 1523. The next year it appeared, with a melody, in the *Etlich Christlich lider* (Wittenberg). The melody with which it is now associated is said to have been written down by Luther from the singing of a travelling artisan. The hymn, with this tune, was first printed in Joseph Klug's *Geistliche Lieder* (Wittenberg: 1535).

Another Bach harmonization of this melody appears in the Edition of 1786 as No. 260. Both Terry and Richter include two harmonizations of different tunes under this name. They are: the Edition of

1785, No. 185, "Nun freut euch Gottes Kinder all' "; and the Edition of 1785, No. 183, "Nun freut euch, lieben Christen g mein". However, since the melody is a different one in each case from the example here presented, they cannot be quoted as harmonizations of this chorale tune.

The instrumentation given for this chorale in the "Christmas Oratorio" is as follows: soprano, *Oboi I & II* and *Violino I;* alto, *Violino II;* tenor, *Viola;* and bass, *Organo e Continuo.* This *Continuo* presents an unusually interesting form, and for this reason it is written out in full.

The organ prelude on this melody is a trio, with *cantus firmus* in the pedal.

The English translation was made for this edition by Albert Riemenschneider.

86. SCHMÜCKE DICH, O LIEBE SEELE

This hymn and melody were first published in Johann Crüger's *Geistliche Kirchen-Melodien* (Leipzig: 1649); the melody is by Crüger.

No other Bach harmonization of this melody is known.

No instrumentation for this chorale is given in the score. For the cantata, the instruments are as follows: *Flauti I & II, Oboe I, Oboe da caccia, Violoncello piccolo,* Strings, and *Continuo.* The latter is not figured.

The organ prelude on this melody, one of the *Eighteen Chorales,* has been the subject of much comment. Schumann said that Mendelssohn told him that if life were to deprive him of hope and faith, this one chorale would bring them back. Schweitzer says it is of the type which might fairly be called "mystic". Parry speaks of Bach's writing *Orgelchoräle* throughout his life, among them "some wonderful human documents of the very greatest fascination, such as 'Schmücke dich' ".

The hymn, by Johann Franck, is for the Holy Communion, and has had wide use in Germany. The translation is from Catherine Winkworth's *Lyra Germanica* (1858).

87. SINGEN WIR AUS HERZENSGRUND

This melody was set to this hymn in Johann Roh's *Gesangbuch* (Frankfurt am Main: 1589). It is evidently a version of the tune printed in the *Gesangbuch der Brüder in Behemen und Merherrn* (Nürnberg: 1544), to Roh's "Da Christus geboren war". In earlier centuries the melody may have been used for the Latin "In natali Domini", upon which Roh's hymn was based.

This appears to be the only harmonization by Bach of this chorale.

The instrumentation is as follows: soprano, *Oboi I & II* and *Violino I;* alto, *Violino II;* tenor, *Viola;* and bass, *Continuo.*

Various sixteenth-century dates have been given for the first appearance of this anonymous hymn, which apparently was first issued on a broadsheet. The translation has been made by Albert Riemenschneider for this edition.

88. VERLEIH' UNS FRIEDEN GNÄDIGLICH

The present setting is a combination of two hymns and two melodies. The first is Luther's "Verleih' uns Frieden", based on the sixth- or seventh-century antiphon "Da pacem, Domine", a hymn of peace which from 1279 was ordered to be sung at every mass before the "Agnus Dei". Luther's translation (prose version in 1527, metrical in 1529) was often sung after the sermon. In 1566 was added the "Gieb unsern Fürsten und aller Obrigkeit". The first melody appeared with the hymn as early as 1531; and it is in Joseph Klug's *Geistliche Lieder* (1535): both are derived from the melody for the antiphon. The second melody was published with the hymn in *Das christlich Kinderlied D. Martini Lutheri* (Wittenberg: 1566). The *Amen* dates from 1573.

The only other Bach harmonization of this melody seems to be in Cantata 126, where it is set to "Verleih' uns Frieden gnädiglich".

The instrumentation in Cantata 42 for this chorale is as follows: soprano, *Oboi I & II* and *Violino I;* alto, *Violino II;* tenor, *Viola;* and bass, *Fagotto* and *Organo e Continuo.*

The English translation was made for this edition by Albert Riemenschneider.

89. WÄR' GOTT NICHT MIT UNS DIESE ZEIT

This melody and hymn were first published in the *Geystliche gesangk Buchleyn* (Wittenberg: 1524). The composer of the melody is not known; some attribute it to Luther, others to Johann Walther.

This is the only harmonization by J. S. Bach of this melody.

The instrumentation is as follows: soprano, *Corno da caccia, Oboi I & II,* and *Violino I;* alto, *Violino II;* tenor, *Viola;* and bass, *Continuo.*

The hymn is Luther's German version of Psalm 124. The English translation by Richard Massie is from his *Martin Luther's Spiritual Songs* (1854).

90. WELT, ADE! ICH BIN DEIN MÜDE

No other harmonization by J. S. Bach of this chorale is known. The present setting, although used by Bach in one of his cantatas, has been traced back to Johann Rosenmüller; it appeared for the first time in Johann Quirsfeld's *Geistlicher Harffen-Klang* (Leipzig: 1679). Since it appeared in Cantata 27 (without change), it was frequently credited to J. S. Bach in the early collections. Zahn said that the whole notes in $\frac{3}{1}$ measure should in no case be longer than the quarters in the $\frac{4}{4}$ measure.

Bach's instrumentation for this chorale in Cantata 27 is as follows: soprano I, *Corno* and *Oboi I & II;* soprano II, *Violino I;* alto, *Violino II;* tenor, *Viola;* and bass, *Continuo* (unfigured).

The hymn was printed on a broadsheet for the funeral of Johanne Magdalene, daughter of the Archidiaconus Abraham Teller, of St. Nicholas' Church, Leipzig, on Feb. 27, 1649. The English translation, by Catherine Winkworth, appeared in her *Lyra Germanica* (1858).

91. WERDE MUNTER, MEIN GEMÜTHE

This melody was composed by Johann Schop for this hymn, and was first published in Rist's *Himlischer Lieder mit Melodeien* (Lüneburg: 1642).

Bach made the following settings of this melody, other than the one here under discussion: in Cantata 55, to the words "Bin ich gleich von dir gewichen"; in Cantata 146, where the words are not indicated in the score; twice in Cantata 147, to the words "Wohl mir, dass ich Jesum habe" and "Jesus bleibet meine Freude" (both these settings have *Tromba, Oboi I & II,* Strings, and *Continuo,* with interludes); in Cantata 154, to the words "Jesu, mein Hort und Erretter". It is also Nos. 349 and 364 in the Edition of 1787.

The instrumentation indicated for the present setting is as follows: soprano, *Flauti traversi I & II, Oboi I & II,* and *Violino I;* alto, *Violino II;* tenor, *Viola;* and bass, *Organo e Continuo.*

In several recent arrangements for piano, Bach's setting from Cantata 147, known in English as "Jesu, Joy of Man's Desiring", has become very popular. This setting will be found as No. 100 in Book II of the present collection.

The words here used are the sixth stanza of Johann Rist's evening hymn, "Werde munter, mein Gemüthe", from the book noted above. The English translation, by Dr. Emanuel Cronenwett, appeared in 1924.

CHORALES No. 1-91 IN OPEN SCORE

Chorales

by
Johann Sebastian Bach*

Selected and Edited by
Charles N. Boyd and Albert Riemenschneider

1. Ach Gott, vom Himmel sieh' darein
"Behold, O Lord, the many foes"

From Cantata 153:
"Schau', lieber Gott"

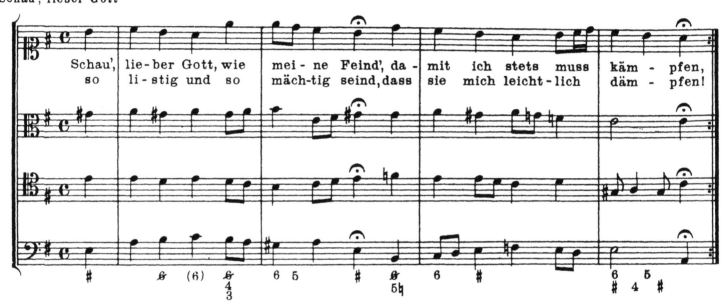

*In the ensuing pages, ninety-one chorales are given first in open score and then in close score. For English translations of the texts, see the close-score versions (pp. 78-127); for the authorship of the texts; see the Notes on the Chorales (pp. x-xxx).

2. Ach Gott, wie manches Herzeleid
"Preserve my faith from error free"

From Cantata 3:
"Ach Gott, wie manches Herzeleid"

Er-halt' mein Herz im Glau-ben rein, so leb' und sterb' ich dir al-lein. Jesu, mein Trost, hör' mein Be-gier': o mein Hei-land, wär' ich be: dir!

3. Auf meinen lieben Gott
"In God, the Lord most just"

From Cantata 188:
"Ich habe meine Zuversicht"

Auf mei-nen lie-ben Gott trau' ich in Angst und Noth; er kann mich all-zeit ret-ten aus
Trüb-sal, Angst und Nö-then, mein Un-glück kann er wen-den, steht all's in sei-nen Hän-den.

4. Aus tiefer Noth schrei ich zu dir
"What though our sins are manifold"

From Cantata 38:
"Aus tiefer Noth"

Ob bei uns ist der Sün-den viel, bei Gott ist viel mehr Gna - de, sein' Hand zu
hel - fen hat kein Ziel, wie gross auch sei der Scha - de. Er ist al - lein der gu - te
Hirt, der I - sra - el er - lö - sen wird aus sei - nen Sün - den al - len.
al - len.

5. Christ ist erstanden
"Alleluia, alleluia, alleluia!"

From Cantata 66:
"Erfreut euch, ihr Herzen"

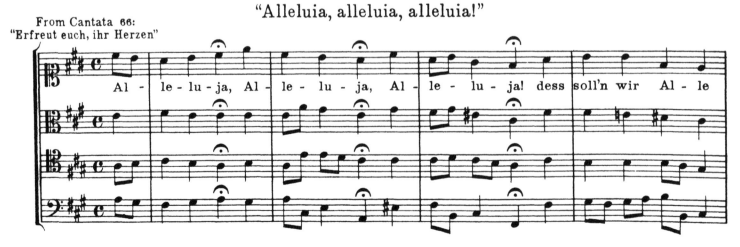

Al - le - lu - ja, Al - le - lu - ja, Al - le - lu - ja! dess soll'n wir Al - le

6. Christ lag in Todesbanden
"With joyful heart we now surround"

From Cantata 4:
"Christ lag in Todesbanden"

7. Christus, der uns selig macht
"Jesus, Source of heavenly light"

From the "St. John Passion"

8. Du Friedefürst, Herr Jesu Christ
"Lord Jesu, blessed Prince of Peace"

From Cantata 67:
"Halt' im Gedächtniss Jesum Christ"

9. Du, o schönes Weltgebäude
"Come, O Death, of Sleep the brother"

From Cantata 56:
"Ich will den Kreuzstab gerne tragen"

Komm, o Tod, du Schla - fes Bru - der, komm, und füh - re mich nur fort;
lö - se mei - nes Schiff - leins Ru - der, brin - ge mich an si - chern Port.

Es mag, wer da will, dich scheu - en, du kannst mich viel - mehr er -

freu - en; denn durch dich komm' ich hin - ein zu dem schön - sten Jé - su - lein.

10. Erschienen ist der herrlich' Tag
"The day hath dawned, the day of days"

From Cantata 67:
"Halt' im Gedächtniss Jesum Christ"

11. Freu' dich sehr, o meine Seele
"Open wide for me the portal"

From Cantata 32:
"Liebster Jesu, mein Verlangen"

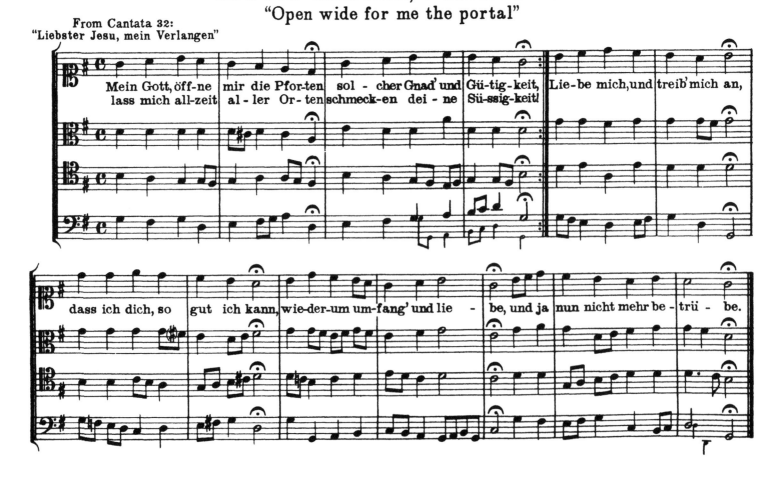

12. Gelobet seist du, Jesu Christ
"All this He did that He might prove"

From Cantata 64:
"Sehet, welch' eine Liebe"

13. Herr Christ, der ein'ge Gottes-Sohn
"Awake us, Lord, we pray to Thee"

From Cantata 96:
"Herr Christ, der ein'ge Gottes-Sohn"

14. Herzlich thut mich verlangen
"Acknowledge me, my Keeper"

From the "St. Matthew Passion"

15. Herzlich thut mich verlangen
"Beside Thee, Lord"

From the "St. Matthew Passion"

16. Herzlich thut mich verlangen
"Commit thy ways, O pilgrim"

From the "St. Matthew Passion"

17. Herzlich thut mich verlangen
"O Head, all bruised and wounded"

From the "St. Matthew Passion"

18. Herzlich thut mich verlangen
"When I too am departing"

From the "St. Matthew Passion"

19. Herzliebster Jesu, was hast du verbrochen
"Alas, dear Lord, what evil hast Thou done now"

From the "St. Matthew Passion"

20. Jesu Leiden, Pein und Tod
"Peter, who doth not recall"

From the "St. John Passion"

21. Jesus, meine Zuversicht
"Wake, my heart"

From Cantata 145:
"So du mit deinem Munde"

Auf, mein Herz! Des Her-ren Tag hat die Nacht der Furcht ver-trie-ben. Chri-stus, der im Gra-be lag,

ist im To-de nicht ge-blie - ben. Nun-mehr bin ich recht ge-tröst't, Je-sus hat die Welt er-löst.

22. Liebster Immanuel, Herzog der Frommen
"Then pass forever now, all empty pleasure"

From Cantata 123:
"Liebster Immanuel, Herzog der Frommen"

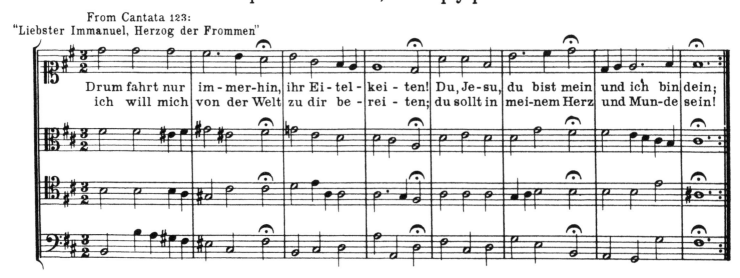

Drum fahrt nur im - mer-hin, ihr Ei - tel - kei - ten! Du, Je-su, du bist mein und ich bin dein;
ich will mich von der Welt zu dir be - rei - ten; du sollt in mei-nem Herz und Mun-de sein!

Mein gan-zes Le-ben sei dir er-ge-ben, bis man mich ein-stens legt in's Grab hin-ein.

23. Lobt Gott, ihr Christen alle gleich
"Today He opens us the door"

From Cantata 151:
"Süsser Trost, mein Jesus kommt"

Heut' schleusst er wie-der auf die Thür zum schö-nen Pa-ra-deis, der

Che-rub steht nicht mehr da-für, Gott sei Lob, Ehr' und Preis,— Gott sei Lob, Ehr' und Preis.

24. Mach's mit mir, Gott, nach deiner Güt'
"Though Thou wert captive, Lord divine"

From the "St. John Passion"

25. Meine Seel' erhebt den Herren
"Glory be to God the Father"

From Cantata 10:
"Meine Seel' erhebt den Herren"

26. Nun komm, der Heiden Heiland
"Praise be God, the Father, done"

From Cantata 62:
"Nun komm, der Heiden Heiland"

27. O Ewigkeit, du Donnerwort
"Eternity, tremendous word"

From Cantata 20:
"O Ewigkeit, du Donnerwort"

28. Preise, Jerusalem, den Herrn
(Herr Gott, dich loben wir)
"Help us, O Lord, from age to age"

From Cantata 119:
"Preise, Jerusalem, den Herrn"

Hilf dei-nem Volk, Herr Je - su Christ, und seg - ne das dein Erb-theil ist. Wart'

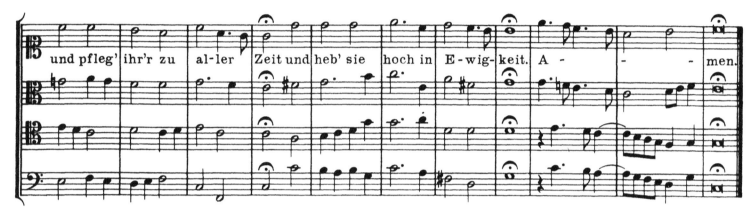

und pfleg' ihr'r zu al-ler Zeit und heb' sie hoch in E-wig-keit. A - - - men.

29. Puer natus in Bethlehem
"And kingly pilgrims, long foretold"

From Cantata 65:
"Sie werden aus Saba Alle kommen"

Die Kön'-ge aus Sa - ba ka-men dar, ka - - men dar, Gold, Weih-rauch,

Myrr - hen brach-ten sie dar, Al - le - lu - ja, Al - le - - lu - ja!

30. Valet will ich dir geben
"When all around is darkling"

From the "St. John Passion"

In mei-nes Her-zens Grun-de, dein Nam' und Kreuz al - lein Er-schein' mir in dem
Fun-kelt all-zeit und Stun-de, drauf kann ich fröh-lich sein.

Bil - de zu Trost in mei-ner Noth, wie du, Herr Christ, so mil - de dich hast ge-blut't zu Tod.

31. Vom Himmel hoch, da komm' ich her
"Behold, there lies in darkened stall"

"Christmas Oratorio", No. 17

Schaut hin! dort liegt im fin - stern Stall, dess' Herr-schaft ge-het ü-ber-all. Da

Spei - se vor-mals sucht' ein Rind, da ru - het jetzt der Jung-frau'n Kind.

Oboe

Oboe

32. Warum sollt' ich mich denn grämen
"Thee, dear Lord, with heed I'll cherish"

"Christmas Oratorio", No. 32

33. Was Gott thut, das ist wohlgethan
"What God does, ever well is done"

From Cantata 144:
"Nimm, was dein ist, und gehe hin"

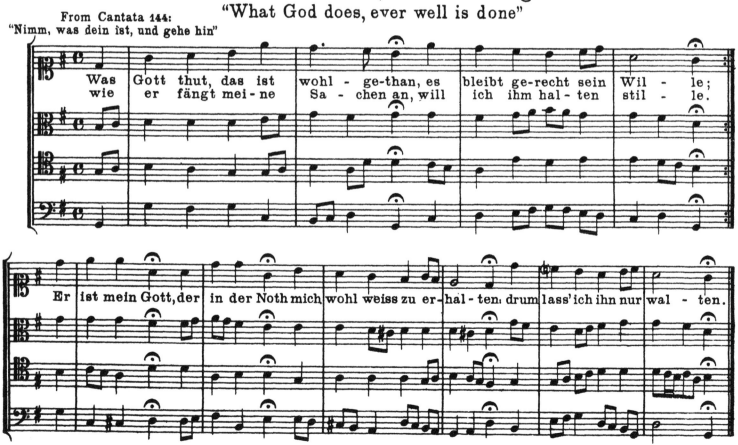

34. Wer nur den lieben Gott lässt walten
"Sing, pray, and keep His ways unswerving"

From Cantata 93:
"Wer nur den lieben Gott lässt walten"

35. Ach, Gott und Herr
"If pain and woe must follow sin"

From Cantata 48:
"Ich elender Mensch"

fahr' hier fort und scho-ne dort, und lass mich hier wohl bü - - - ssen.

36. Ach, lieben Christen, seid getrost
(Wo Gott der Herr nicht bei uns hält)
"'Wake or asleep, in life or death"

From Cantata 114:
"Ach, lieben Christen, seid getrost"

Wir wa - chen o - der schla-fen ein, so sind wir doch des Her - ren;
auf Chri - stum wir ge - tau-fet sein, der kann dem Sa - tan weh - ren.

Durch A-dam auf uns kömmt der Tod, Chri-stus hilft uns aus al-ler Noth. Drum lo-ben wir den Her - ren.

37. Ach wie flüchtig, ach wie nichtig
"O how futile, how inutile"

From Cantata 26:
"Ach wie flüchtig"

Ach wie flüch-tig, ach wie nich-tig sind der Men-schen Sa - chen! Al-les, Al - les

was wir se-hen, das muss fal-len und ver-ge-hen; wer Gott fürcht't, bleibt e - wig ste-hen.

38. Alle Menschen müssen sterben
"Yes, methinks I now behold it"

From Cantata 162:
"Ach, ich sehe, jetzt da ich zur Hochzeit gehe"

Ach, ich ha - be schon er - bli - cket die - se gro - sse Herr-lich-keit!

Jetz-und werd' ich schön ge-schmü-cket mit dem wei-ssen Him-mels-kleid, mit der guld'nen Eh-ren-kro-ne

steh' ich da für Got-tes Thro-ne, schau-e sol-che Freu-de an, die kein En-de neh-men kann!

39. Das neugebor'ne Kindelein
"He brings the year of jubilee"

From Cantata 122:
"Das neugebor'ne Kindelein"

Es bringt das rech - te Ju-bel-jahr, was trau-ern wir denn im-mer-dar?

Frisch auf! itzt ist___ es Sin-gens-zeit, das Je-su-lein___ wend't al-les Leid.

wend't al - les

wend't al - les

wend't al - les

40. Durch Adams Fall ist ganz verderbt

"I send my cries unto the Lord"

From Cantata 18:
"Gleich wie der Regen und Schnee"

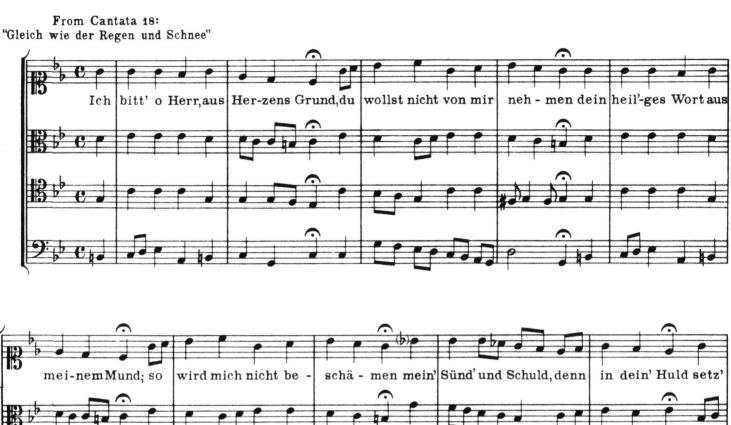

Ich bitt' o Herr, aus Her-zens Grund, du wollst nicht von mir neh - men dein heil'-ges Wort aus

mei-nem Mund; so wird mich nicht be - schä - men mein' Sünd' und Schuld, denn in dein' Huld setz'

ich all mein Ver-trau - en. Wer sich nur fest da-rauf ver-lässt, der wird den Tod nicht schau - en.

41. Ein' feste Burg ist unser Gott

"Still shall they leave that word His might"

From Cantata 80:
"Ein' feste Burg"

42. Erhalt' uns, Herr, bei deinem Wort
"Assert Thy power with all speed"

From Cantata 6:
"Bleib' bei uns, denn es will Abend werden"

43. Ermuntre dich, mein schwacher Geist
"Break forth, O lovely morning light"

"Christmas Oratorio", No. 12

dass die-ses schwa-che Knä-be-lein soll un-ser Trost und Freu-de sein, dazu den Sa-tan zwin-gen und letzt-lich Frie-den brin-gen.

44. Es ist das Heil uns kommen her
"Be not cast down when He delays"

From Cantata 9:
"Es ist das Heil uns kommen her"

Ob sich's an-liess, als wollt' er nicht, lass dich es nicht er-schre-cken,
Denn wo er ist am be-sten mit, da will er's nicht ent-de-cken;

sein Wort lass dir ge-wis-ser sein, und ob dein Herz spräch lau-ter Nein, so lass doch dir nicht grau-en.

45. Es ist genug: Herr, wenn es dir gefällt
"It is enough! Lord, by Thy wise decree"

From Cantata 60:
"O Ewigkeit, du Donnerwort"

46. Gott des Himmels und der Erden
"For the inmost heart-recesses"

"Christmas Oratorio", No. 53

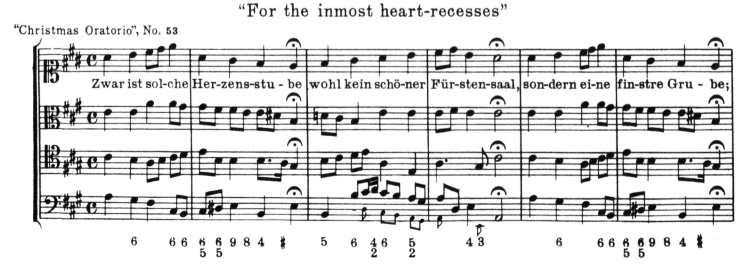

doch, so-bald dein Gna-den-strahl in die-sel-be nur wird blin-ken, wird sie vol-ler Son-nen dün-ken.

47. Helft mir Gott's Güte preisen
"These mercies we're adoring"

From Cantata 16:
"Herr Gott dich loben wir"

All solch dein Güt' wir prei - sen, Va - ter in's Him-mels Thron, Die

du uns thust be - wei - sen durch Je - sum dei - nen Sohn, und bit-ten fer - ner dich, gieb

uns ein fried-lich Jah - re, vor al-les Leid be - wah - re und nähr' uns mil-dig-lich.

48. Herr Gott, dich loben wir
"O help us, Lord, Thy servants crowned"

From Cantata 120:
"Gott, man lobet dich in der Stille"

Nun hilf uns, Herr, den Die-nern dein, die mit dein'm Blut er- lö-set sein. Lass' uns im Him-mel ha-ben Theil mit den Heil'-gen im ew'-gen Heil. Hilf dei-nem Volk, Herr Je- su Christ, und seg- ne, was dein Erb-theil ist; wart' und pfleg' ihr'r zu al-ler Zeit und heb' sie hoch in E-wig-keit.

49. Herr Jesu Christ, du höchstes Gut
"Lord Jesus Christ, my only Stay"

From Cantata 48:
"Ich elender Mensch"

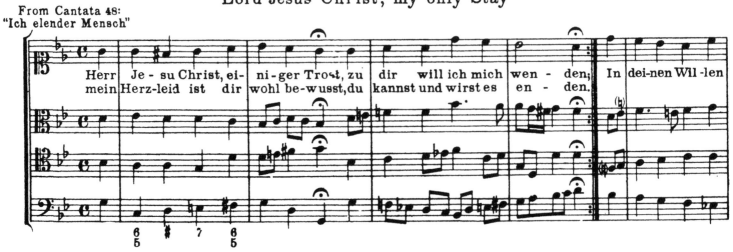

Herr Je - su Christ, ei- ni-ger Trost, zu dir will ich mich wen - den; In dei-nen Wil -len
mein Herz-leid ist dir wohl be-wusst, du kannst und wirst es en - den.

sei's ge-stellt, mach's, lie-ber Gott, wie dir's ge-fällt: dein bin und will ich blei- -ben.

50. Herr Jesu Christ, wahr'r Mensch und Gott
"O Lord, forgive our sins so great"

From Cantata 127:
"Herr Jesu Christ, wahr'r Mensch und Gott"

Ach Herr, ver-gieb all' un-sre Schuld, hilf, dass wir war-ten mit Ge-duld, bis un-ser Stünd-lein kömmt her-bei, auch un-ser Glaub' stets wa-cker sei, dein'm Wort zu trau-en fe-stig-lich, bis wir ein-schla-fen se-lig-lich.

51. Herr, wie du will't, so schick's mit mir
"Lord, as Thou wilt, deal Thou with me"

From Cantata 156:
"Ich steh' mit einem Fuss im Grabe"

Herr, wie du will't, so schick's mit mir im Le-ben und_____ im Ster - ben; al -

lein zu dir steht mein Be-gehr, Herr, lass mich nicht_____ ver-der - ben! Er -

halt' mich nur in deiner Huld, sonst, wie du will't, gieb mir Ge-duld; dein Will' der ist_____ der be - ste.

52. Ich freue mich in dir
"'Tis well! no more lament!"

From Cantata 133:
"Ich freue mich in dir"

53. Jesu, der du meine Seele
"I believe, Lord; help my frailty"

From Cantata 78:
"Jesu, der du meine Seele"

Herr! ich glau-be, hilf mir Schwachen, lass mich ja ver-za-gen nicht; du, du kannst mich stär-ker ma-chen, wenn mich Sünd' und Tod an-ficht. Dei-ner Gü-te will ich trau-en, bis ich fröh-lich wer-de schau-en dich, Herr Je-su, nach dem Streit in der sü-ssen E-wig-keit.

54. Kommt her zu mir, spricht Gottes Sohn
"No child of man upon this earth"

From Cantata 74:
"Wer mich liebet, der wird mein Wort halten"

Kein Men-schen-kind hier auf der Erd' ist die-ser ed-len Ga-be werth, bei

55. Mit Fried' und Freud' ich fahr' dahin
"He is the Hope, the Saving Light"

From Cantata 83:
"Erfreute Zeit im neuen Bunde"

56. Nun lasst uns Gott dem Herren
"His Word, Baptism, and Sacrament"

From Cantata 165:
"O heil'ges Geist- und Wasserbad"

Sein Wort, sein' Tau - fe, sein Nachtmahl dient wi - der al - len Un - fall, der

heil' - ge Geist im Glau - ben lehrt uns da - rauf ver - trau - en.

57. Nun lob', mein' Seel', den Herren
"For, as a tender father"

From Cantata 17:
"Wer Dank opfert, der preiset mich"

Wie sich ein Vat'r er - bar - met üb'r sei - ne jun - ge Kind-lein klein:
So thut der Herr uns Ar - men, so wir ihn kind - lich fürchten rein.

58. O Gott, du frommer Gott
"And grant me, Lord, to do"

From Cantata 45:
"Es ist dir gesagt, Mensch"

Gieb, dass ich thu' mit Fleiss, was mir zu thun ge-büh-ret, wo-
zu mich dein Be-fehl in mei-nem Stan-de füh-ret. Gieb, dass ich's thu-e bald, zu
der Zeit, da ich soll; und wenn ich's thu', so gieb, dass es ge-ra-the wohl.

59. O Herre Gott, dein göttlich Wort
"My trust is bold"

From Cantata 184:
"Erwünschtes Freudenlicht"

Herr, ich hoff' je, du wer-dest die in kei-ner Noth ver-las - - sen,
die dein Wort recht als treu-e Knecht' im Herz'n und Glau-ben fas - - sen;

giebst ihn'n be-reit die Se-lig-keit und läss't sie nicht ver-der-ben. O

Herr, durch dich bitt' ich, lass mich fröh-lich und se-lig ster-ben.

60. O Welt, ich muss dich lassen
(Nun ruhen alle Wälder)
"Who could so rudely smite Thee"

From the "St. Matthew Passion"

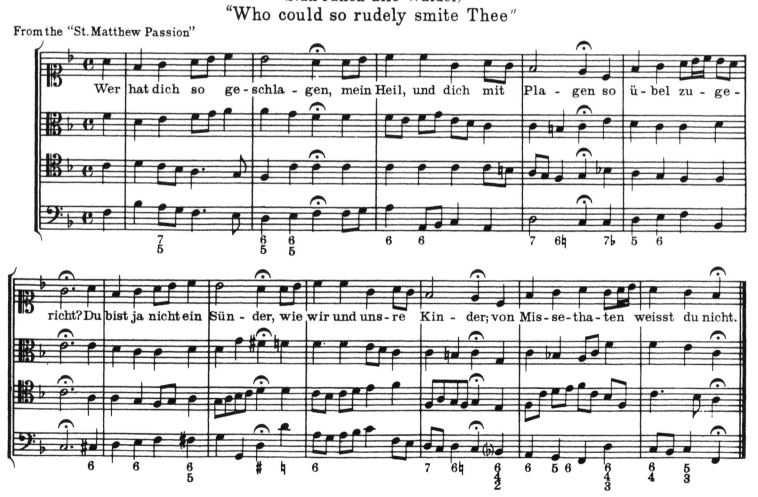

Wer hat dich so ge-schla-gen, mein Heil, und dich mit Pla-gen so ü-bel zu-ge-

richt? Du bist ja nicht ein Sün-der, wie wir und uns-re Kin-der; von Mis-se-tha-ten weisst du nicht.

61. Schwing' dich auf zu deinem Gott
"Lift thy head and proudly sing"

From Cantata 40:
"Dazu ist erschienen der Sohn Gottes"

Schüt-tle dei-nen Kopf und sprich: fleuch, du al-te Schlan-ge! was er-neurst du dei-nen Stich, machst mir angst und ban-ge? Ist dir doch der Kopf zer-knickt, und ich bin durch's Lei-den mei-nes Hei-lands dir ent-rückt in den Saal der Freu-den.

62. Straf mich nicht in deinem Zorn
"Let us watch then, pray with heed"

From Cantata 115:
"Mache dich, mein Geist, bereit"

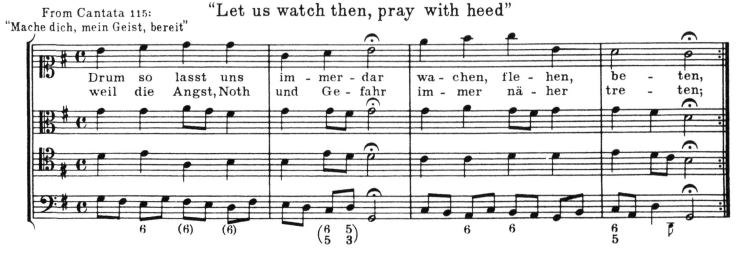

Drum so lasst uns im-mer-dar wa-chen, fle-hen, be-ten,
weil die Angst, Noth und Ge-fahr im-mer nä-her tre-ten;

63. Vater unser im Himmelreich
"Thy will be done on earth, O Lord"

From the "St. John Passion"

64. Von Gott will ich nicht lassen
"This is the Father's pleasure"

From Cantata 73:
"Herr, wie du willt, so schick's mit mir"

Das ist des Va-ters Wil - le, der uns er-schaf-fen hat; sein Sohn hat Gut's die
Fül - le er-wor-ben uns aus Gnad; auch Gott, der heil'-ge Geist, im Glau-ben uns re -
gie - ret, zum Reich des Him - mels füh - ret: ihm sei Lob, Ehr' und Preis.

65. Wachet auf, ruft uns die Stimme
"Glory unto Thee be given"

From Cantata 140:
"Wachet auf, ruft uns die Stimme"

Glo - ri - a sei dir ge - sun - gen mit Men-schen-
Von zwölf Per - len sind die Pfor - ten an dei - ner

Glo - ri - a sei
Von zwölf Per-len

66. Warum betrübst du dich, mein Herz

"What here may shine"

From Cantata 47:
"Wer sich selbst erhöhet"

67. Was mein Gott will, das g'scheh' allzeit

"What my God wills is best alway"

From Cantata 72:
"Alles nur nach Gottes Willen"

Er hilft aus Noth, der from-me Gott, und züch-ti-get mit Ma - ssen. Wer

Gott ver-traut, fest auf ihn baut, den will er nicht ver-las - - sen.

68. Wir Christenleut'
"Sin brought us grief"

From Cantata 40:
"Dazu ist erschienen der Sohn Gottes"

Die Sünd' macht Leid, die Sünd' macht Leid; Chri-stus bringt Freud', weil er zu Trost in die-se Welt ge-

kom-men. Mit uns ist Gott nun in der Noth: wer ist, der uns als Chri-sten kann ver-dam-men?

69. Allein zu dir, Herr Jesu Christ

"Glory to God in highest heaven"

From Cantata 33:
'Allein zu dir, Herr Jesu Christ"

70. Christ, unser Herr, zum Jordan kam
"So that we, all with one accord"

From Cantata 176:
"Es ist ein trotzig und verzagt Ding"

71. Christum wir sollen loben schon
"Honor to Thee, O Christ, be paid"

From Cantata 121:
"Christum wir sollen loben schon"

Lob, Ehr' und Dank ___ sei dir ge-sagt, Christ ge-bor'n von ___ der rei-nen

Magd, sammt Va - - -ter und dem heil' - - - - gen Geist von

nun an bis ___ in E - - -wig-keit.
in E - - - - - - - - - -wig-keit.
in E - - -wig-keit, in E - - - -wig-keit.
in E - - - - - - - -wig-keit.

72. Freu' dich sehr, o meine Seele

"For the Baptist's voice is crying"

From Cantata 30:
"Freue dich, erlöste Schaar"

73. Freuet euch, ihr Christen
"Jesu, guard and guide Thy members"

From Cantata 40:
"Dazu ist erschienen der Sohn Gottes"

Je-su, nimm dich dei - ner Glie-der fer - ner in Ge - na - den an; schen-ke, was man

bit - ten kann, zu er - qui - cken dei - ne Brü-der: gieb der gan-zen Chri - sten-schaar

Frie-den und ein sel-ges Jahr! Freu-de, Freu-de ü - ber Freu-de! Chri-stus weh-ret

al - lem Lei-de. Won-ne, Won-ne ü - ber Won-ne! er ist die Ge - na-den-son-ne.

74. Herzlich lieb hab' ich dich, o Herr

"O Lord, I love Thee from my heart"

From Cantata 174:
"Ich liebe den Höchsten von ganzem Gemüthe"

75. Ich dank' dir, lieber Herre
"True faith to me vouchsafe, Lord"

From Cantata 37:
"Wer da glaubet und getauft wird"

76. Ist Gott mein Schild und Helfersmann
"With God my guard and shepherd true"

From Cantata 85:
"Ich bin ein guter Hirt"

Ist Gott mein Schutz und treu - er Hirt, kein Un-glück mich be - rüh - ren wird; weicht,

al - le mei - ne Fein - de, die ihr mir stif-tet Angst und Pein, es wird zu eu - rem

Scha - den sein; ich ha - be Gott zum Freun - de, ich ha - be Gott zum Freun - de.

77. Jesu, meine Freude
"Jesus, priceless Treasure"

From Motet 3:
'Jesu, meine Freude"

Je - su, mei - ne Freu - de, mei - nes Her-zens Wei - de, Je - su, mei - ne Zier,

ach, wie lang', ach, lan - ge ist dem Her-zen ban - ge, und ver-langt nach dir!

Got-tes Lamm, mein Bräu - ti-gam, au-sser dir soll mir auf Er - den nichts sonst Lie-bers wer - den.

78. Jesu, meine Freude

"In Thine arms I rest me"

From Motet 3:
"Jesu, meine Freude"

79. Jesu, meine Freude
"Hence with earthly treasure!"

From Motet 3:
"Jesu, meine Freude"

80. Jesu, meine Freude
"Fare thee well that errest"

From Motet 3:
"Jesu, meine Freude"

81. Jesu, meine Freude
"Hence, all fears and sadness!"

From Motet 3:
"Jesu, meine Freude"

Weicht, ihr Trau - er - gei - ster, denn mein Freu-den- mei - ster, Je - sus, tritt her - ein.

De - nen, die Gott lie - ben, muss auch ihr Be - trü - ben lau - ter Zu- cker sein.

Duld' ich schon hier Spott und Hohn, den-noch bleibst du auch im Lei - de, Je-su, mei - ne Freu - de.

82. Komm, Jesu, komm
"I give myself into Thy pleasure"

From Motet 5:
"Komm, Jesu, komm"

83. Liebster Gott, wann werd' ich sterben?

"Ruler over dead and living"

From Cantata 8:
"Liebster Gott, wann werd' ich sterben?"

84. Nun bitten wir den heiligen Geist
"Thou sweetest Love! pray we heartily"

From Cantata 197 (Wedding Cantata)
"Gott ist uns're Zuversicht"

85. Nun freut euch, lieben Christen g'mein
"I stand beside Thy manger here"

"Christmas Oratorio," No. 59

Ich steh' an dei-ner Krip-pen hier, o Je-su-lein, mein Le - ben, ich

Je - su-lein,

ORGANO E CONTINUO

komme, bring' und schen-ke dir, was du mir hast ge-ge - ben, Nimm hin, es ist mein

du mir

Geist und Sinn, Herz, Seel' und Muth, nimm Al-les hin, und lass dir's wohl ge-fal - len!

86. Schmücke dich, o liebe Seele
"Jesus, Bread of life from heaven"

From Cantata 180:
"Schmücke dich, o liebe Seele"

87. Singen wir aus Herzensgrund
"God, Who ordained the earth so fair"

From Cantata 187:
"Es wartet Alles auf dich"

88. Verleih' uns Frieden gnädiglich
"Grant us Thy peace, we pray Thee, Lord"

From Cantata 42:
"Am Abend aber desselbigen Sabbaths"

89. Wär' Gott nicht mit uns diese Zeit
"Thanks be to God, Who from the pit"

From Cantata 14:
"Wär' Gott nicht mit uns diese Zeit"

90. Welt, ade! ich bin dein müde

"World, farewell! Of thee I'm tired"

From Cantata 27:
"Wer weiss, wie nahe mir mein Ende"

91. Werde munter, mein Gemüthe
"Though I lapsed, and straying wander"

From the "St. Matthew Passion"

CHORALES No. 1-91 IN CLOSE SCORE

Chorales
by
Johann Sebastian Bach*

1. Ach Gott, vom Himmel sieh' darein
"Behold, O Lord, the many foes"

Be - hold, O Lord, the man - y foes, With whom I strug - gle ev - er:
'Gainst man - y and such might - y woes, My strength a - vail - eth nev - er.

Thy grace my on - ly true sup - port, Though Dev - il, World, and Flesh con - sort, Do Thou my soul de - liv - er.

2. Ach Gott, wie manches Herzeleid
"Preserve my faith from error free"

Pre - serve my faith from er - ror free, That I may live and die in Thee; My

Sav - ior, grant me my de - sire: Let me be Thine when I ex - pire.

*For the German texts, see the open-score versions (pp. 2-76); for the authorship of the translations, see the Notes on the Chorales (pp. x-xxx).

3. Auf meinen lieben Gott
"In God, the Lord most just"

In God, the Lord most just, I place my on - ly trust; For He is my Re - deem - er From sin and the Blas - phem - er. He can and will re - lieve____ me From what may hurt and grieve me.

4. Aus tiefer Noth schrei ich zu dir
"What though our sins are manifold"

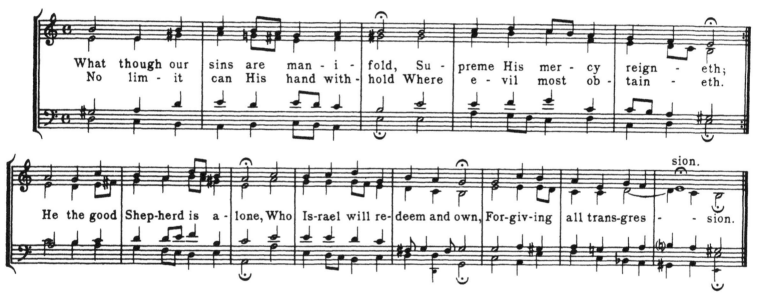

What though our sins are man - i - fold, Su - preme His mer - cy reign - eth;
No lim - it can His hand with - hold Where e - vil most ob - tain - eth.

He the good Shep-herd is a - lone, Who Is-rael will re-deem and own, For-giv-ing all trans-gres - - sion.

5. Christ ist erstanden
"Alleluia, alleluia, alleluia!"

Al - le - lu - ia, al - le - lu - ia, al - le - lu - ia! Re - joice we all to - geth - er, For Christ is our Re - deem - er. Ky - ri - e____ e - leis! Ky - ri - e e - leis!

6. Christ lag in Todesbanden
"With joyful heart we now surround"

With joy-ful heart we now sur-round The hal-lowed East-er ta - - ble,
The Word of Grace doth now con-found The leav- en old, un -sta - - ble. Christ a-lone will

be our food, For hun-gry souls the live-li-hood: In faith none else is ten - a - ble. Al - le - lu - ia!
Al - le - lu - ia!
Al - le - lu - ia!

7. Christus, der uns selig macht
"Jesus, Source of heavenly light"

Je-sus, Source of heav'n-ly light, Nev-er was mis- tak-en: He, who for us in the night As a thief was tak- en,

Led be-fore a god-less throng, False-ly was in - dict - ed, Mocked,de-rid-ed, spat up-on, As Ho-ly Writ cit - - ed.
cit - ed.

8. Du Friedefürst, Herr Jesu Christ
"Lord Jesu, blessed Prince of Peace"

Lord Je - su, bless- ed Prince of Peace, True God, and ver - y Man!
By Thee our hu - man troub- les cease, Whose life is but a span.

Thy sav-ing Name Is what we claim Be-fore Thy heav'n - - ly Fa - ther.

9. Du, o schönes Weltgebäude
"Come, O Death, of Sleep the brother"

Come, O Death, of Sleep the broth - er,
For my bark, be thou the rud - der:
Come, and lead me gent - ly home;
Bring me safe through spray and foam.

He who will may fear thee sore - ly;
Joy thou bring-est me most tru - ly:
Thou shalt lead me through the gates;
Je-sus, Sav-ior, there a-waits.

10. Erschienen ist der herrlich' Tag
"The day hath dawned, the day of days"

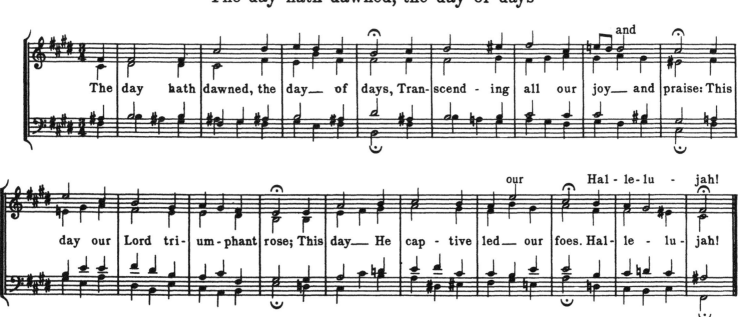

The day hath dawned, the day_ of days, Tran-scend - ing all our joy_ and praise: This

day our Lord tri-um-phant rose; This day_ He cap - tive led_ our foes. Hal - le - lu - jah!

11. Freu' dich sehr, o meine Seele
"Open wide for me the portal"

12. Gelobet seist du, Jesu Christ
"All this He did that He might prove"

13. Herr Christ, der ein'ge Gottes-Sohn
"Awake us, Lord, we pray to Thee"

So will we al-ways thank Thee, That show'st us so great mer - cy And our sins dost for - give.

14. Herzlich thut mich verlangen
"Acknowledge me, my Keeper"

Ac- | knowl-edge me, my | Keep - er; My | Shep-herd, own me | Thine. | | Thy | love full oft hath
Thou | Fount of bless-ings, | deep - er Than | deep-est want of | mine, |

fed __ me With | milk and an-gel- | food; Thy | spir-it still hath | led __ me The | way of heav'n-ly | good.

15. Herzlich thut mich verlangen
"Beside Thee, Lord"

Be - | side Thee, Lord, I've | tak - en My | place—for-bid me | not! | | If | pain's last pale-ness
Hence | will I ne'er be | shak - en Though | Thou to death be | brought. |

hold __ Thee, In | ag - o - ny op - | pressed, Then, | then will I en - | fold Thee With- | in this arm and | breast.

16. Herzlich thut mich verlangen
"Commit thy ways, O pilgrim"

Com-mit thy ways, O pil-grim On time's dark, storm-y seas,
To Him who or-ders all things Through sweet e-ter-ni-ties, Who mea-sures out their
cours-es To clouds, winds, waves be-low; He too will find a path-way Where-in thy feet may go.

17. Herzlich thut mich verlangen
"O Head, all bruised and wounded"

O Head, all bruised and wound-ed, Hung up to bru-tal scorn! O Head, to hon-or
O Head, for shame sur-round-ed With crown of cru-el thorn!
wont-ed, To splen-dor all div-ine, Now out-raged and af-front-ed: All hail, dear Mas-ter mine!

18. Herzlich thut mich verlangen
"When I too am departing"

When I too am de-part-ing, Then part Thou not from me:
On death's lone jour-ney start-ing, My soul will feel for Thee. When near my end I

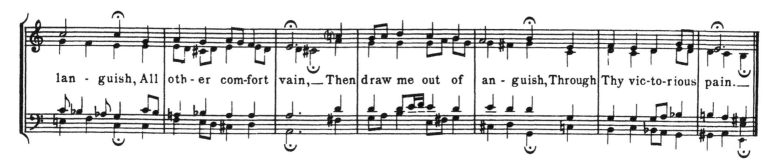

lan - guish, All oth - er com-fort vain,— Then draw me out of an - guish, Through Thy vic-to-rious pain.—

19. Herzliebster Jesu, was hast du verbrochen
"Alas, dear Lord, what evil hast Thou done now"

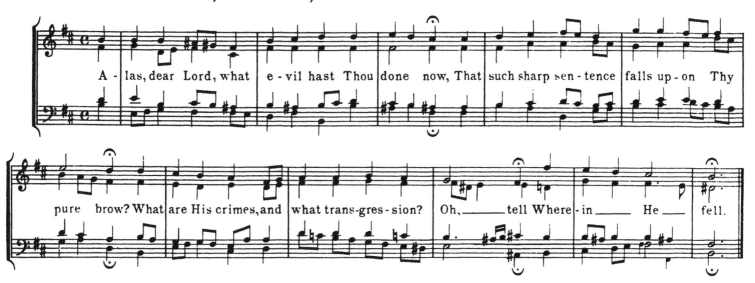

A - las, dear Lord, what e - vil hast Thou done now, That such sharp sen - tence falls up - on Thy

pure brow? What are His crimes, and what trans-gres-sion? Oh,— tell Where - in — He — fell.

20. Jesu Leiden, Pein und Tod
"Peter, who doth not recall"

Pe - ter, who doth not re - call, Hence his God de - ni - eth;

When God's glance doth him ap-pall, Bit-ter-ly he cri - eth. Je - sus, pray Thee, look on me

When through sin I sick - en; Should I from Thy pres-ence flee, Make me con-science-strick en.

21. Jesus, meine Zuversicht
"Wake, my heart"

Wake, my heart; for night of fear Yields to God's own day vic - to - rious.
Christ is ris'n from grave so drear, Reigns in heav'n's do - main, all - glo - rious.

Con - so - la - tion full is mine: Je - sus, Sav - ior, is di - vine.

22. Liebster Immanuel, Herzog der Frommen
"Then pass forever now, all empty pleasure"

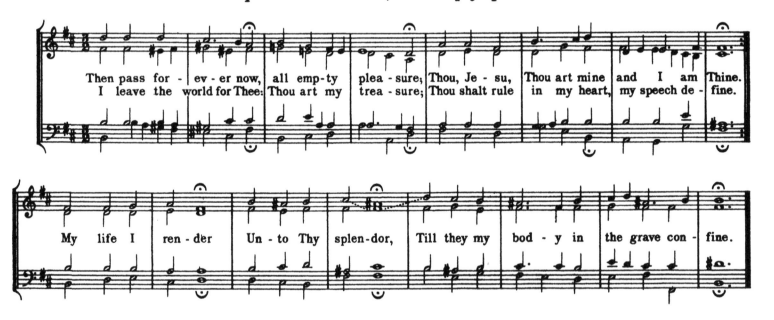

Then pass for - ev - er now, all emp - ty plea - sure; Thou, Je - su, Thou art mine and I am Thine.
I leave the world for Thee: Thou art my trea - sure; Thou shalt rule in my heart, my speech de - fine.

My life I ren - der Un - to Thy splen - dor, Till they my bod - y in the grave con - fine.

23. Lobt Gott, ihr Christen alle gleich
"Today He opens us the door"

To - day He o - pens us the door Of bliss - ful Par - a - dise; The

cher-ub threat-ens there no more; Then let His prais-es rise,——Then let His prais-es rise!

24. Mach's mit mir, Gott, nach deiner Güt'
"Though Thou wert captive, Lord divine"

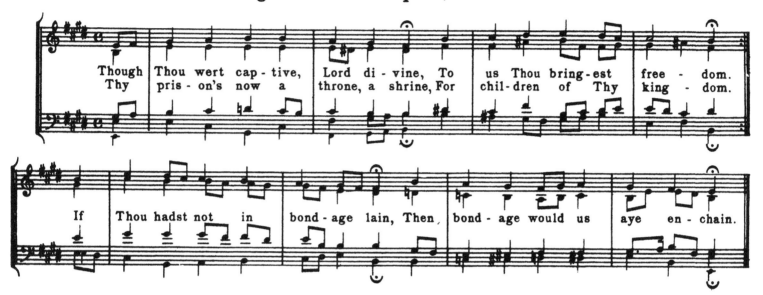

Though Thou wert cap-tive, Lord di-vine, To us Thou bring-est free-dom.
Thy pris-on's now a throne, a shrine, For chil-dren of Thy king-dom.

If Thou hadst not in bond-age lain, Then bond-age would us aye en-chain.

25. Meine Seel' erhebt den Herren
"Glory be to God the Father"

Glo-ry be to God the Fa-ther and the Son, And—— to the Ho-

ly—— Ghost, As it was in the be-gin-ning, And is now,

As it was in the be-gin-ning, And is now, And for-

And for-ev-er-

And for- ev-er-more shall be. A - - - men.——
ev-er-more,—— ev-er shall be. A - - men.

more, ev - er shall be. A - - - - - men.

26. Nun komm, der Heiden Heiland
"Praise be God, the Father, done"

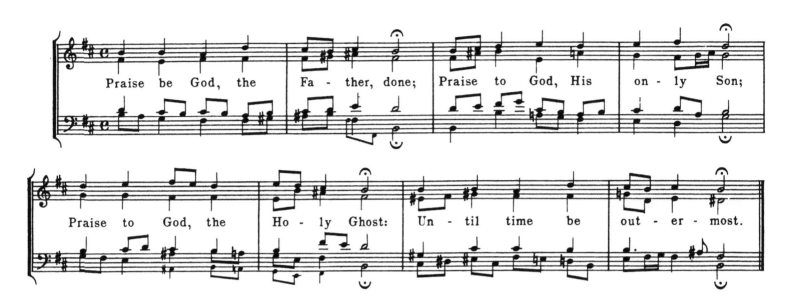

Praise be God, the Father, done; Praise to God, His only Son;

Praise to God, the Holy Ghost: Until time be outermost.

27. O Ewigkeit, du Donnerwort
"Eternity, tremendous word"

Eternity, tremendous word, Home-striking point, heartpiercing sword, Be-
Eternity without a shore, Where ever fiery billows roar, What

ginning without ending!
is thy sight portending? Lord Jesu, when it pleases Thee, Bring me to blest eternity.

28. Preise, Jerusalem, den Herrn
(Herr Gott, dich loben wir)
"Help us, O Lord, from age to age"

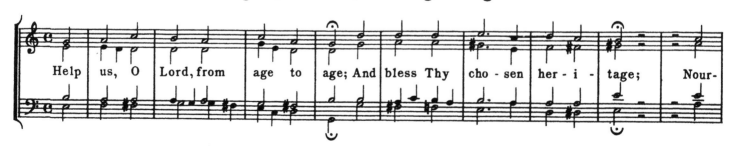

Help us, O Lord, from age to age; And bless Thy chosen heritage; Nour-

ish and keep them by Thy pow'r; And lift them up for - ev - er - more. A - - - men.

29. Puer natus in Bethlehem
"And kingly pilgrims, long foretold"

And king - ly pil - grims, long fore - told, Al - le - lu - ia! From east bring
Al - - le - lu -
Al - le - lu -

in - cense, myrrh, and gold. Al - le - lu - ia! Al le - - lu - ia.

30. Valet will ich dir geben
"When all around is darkling"

When all a - round is dark - ling, Thy name and cross, still bright,
Deep in my heart are spark - ling, Like stars in dark - est night;

Ap - pear Thou in Thy

sor - row, For Thine was woe in - deed, And from Thy cross I bor - row All com-fort heart can need.

31. Vom Himmel hoch, da komm' ich her
"Behold, there lies in darkened stall"

Be - hold, there lies in dark-ened stall Whose heav'n - ly rule will guide us all. Where

ox and ass once sought their food, There rests the Child so pure and good.

32. Warum sollt' ich mich denn grämen
"Thee, dear Lord, with heed I'll cherish"

Thee, dear Lord, with heed I'll cher - ish, Live to Thee, And, with Thee Dy-ing, shall not per -

ish, But shall dwell with Thee for - ev - er, Far on high In the joy That can al-ter nev - er.

33. Was Gott thut, das ist wohlgethan
"What God does, ever well is done"

What God does, ev - er well is done; His will is just and ho - ly;
As He di - rects my sands to run, My spir - it shall keep low - ly.

He is my God; Though sore the rod, His care doth e'er en - fold me: Then He may guide and hold me.

34. Wer nur den lieben Gott lässt walten
"Sing, pray, and keep His ways unswerving"

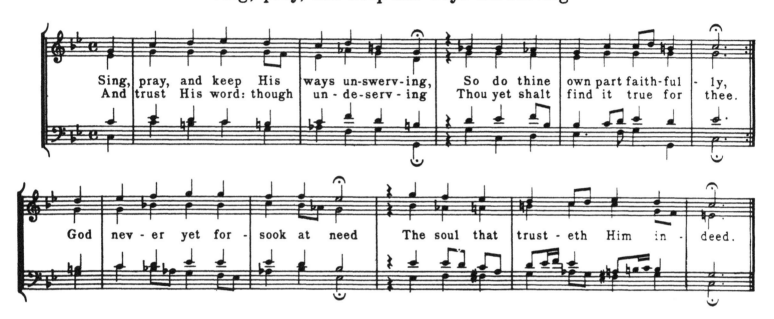

Sing, pray, and keep His ways un-swerv-ing, So do thine own part faith-ful - ly,
And trust His word: though un - de-serv - ing Thou yet shalt find it true for thee.

God nev - er yet for - sook at need The soul that trust - eth Him in - deed.

35. Ach, Gott und Herr
"If pain and woe must follow sin"

If pain and woe must fol - low sin, Then be my path still rough - er: Here
spare me not; if heav'n I win, On earth I glad-ly suf - - - - fer.

36. Ach, lieben Christen, seid getrost
(Wo Gott der Herr nicht bei uns hält)
"'Wake or asleep, in life or death"

'Wake or a-sleep, in life or death, We are in God's pos-ses - sion:
Bap-tized in Christ, we're brought by faith T'ap-proach God's hab - i - ta - tion.

What we have lost in Ad - am's fall Christ hath re - cov - ered

for us all: Praised be the Lord of mer - cy!

37. Ach wie flüchtig, ach wie nichtig
"O how futile, how inutile"

O how fu-tile, how in - u-tile, All, yes all, that's earth - y! Ev - 'ry-thing is

fad - ing, fly - ing; Man is mor-tal; earth is dy-ing: Chris-tian, live, on heav'n re - ly - ing.

38. Alle Menschen müssen sterben
"Yes, methinks I now behold it"

39. Das neugebor'ne Kindelein
"He brings the year of jubilee"

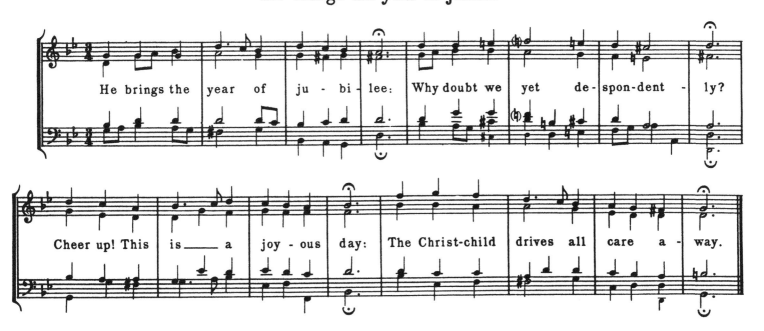

40. Durch Adams Fall ist ganz verderbt

"I send my cries unto the Lord"

I send my cries un-to the Lord; My heart im-plores His fa-vor:
To grant me of His liv-ing Word A nev-er-fail-ing sa-vor;
That sin and shame May lose the claim To hin-der my sal-va-tion; In
Christ, the scope Of all my hope, I 'scape death and dam-na-tion.

41. Ein' feste Burg ist unser Gott

"Still shall they leave that word His might"

Still shall they leave that word His might And yet no thanks shall mer-it;
Still is He with us in the fight, By His good gifts and spir-it.
E'en should they take our life, Wealth, name, child, and wife: Tho' all these be——
gone, Yet noth-ing have they won; God's king-dom ours a-bid-eth.

42. Erhalt' uns, Herr, bei deinem Wort
"Assert Thy power with all speed"

As - sert Thy pow - er with all speed, That Thou art Lord of Lords in - deed; Pro-

tect Thy church most gra - cious - ly, That we may thank Thee con - stant - ly.

43. Ermuntre dich, mein schwacher Geist
"Break forth, O lovely morning light"

Break forth, O love - ly morn - ing light, There - by the heav - ens light - ing.
Ye shep - herd folk, do not take fright Be - cause of an - gels' cit - ing

That this so weak and low - ly child Will be our hope and Sav - ior mild, Will

bonds of Sa - tan sev - er, And bring us peace for - ev - er.

44. Es ist das Heil uns kommen her
"Be not cast down when He delays"

Be not cast down when He de-lays To crown thine ex-pec-ta-tion;
He then is near-est, when thy ways Seem full of des-o-la-tion.

On His e-ter-nal Word re-ly, E'en though thy wa-v'ring heart de-ny; And trust in thy Re-deem-er.

45. Es ist genug: Herr, wenn es dir gefällt
"It is enough! Lord, by Thy wise decree"

It is e-nough! Lord, by Thy wise de-cree I gird me to de-part. My

Je-sus comes! Fare-well, O world, to thee; I seek my heav'n-ly home. In peace I trav-el sure-ly

on-ward; Be-hind is earth-ly grief and sor-row; It is e-nough, it is e-nough!

46. Gott des Himmels und der Erden
"For the inmost heart-recesses"

For the in-most heart-re-cess-es Are not roy-al halls su-preme;
Rath-er are they deep, dark plac-es: But when-e'er Thy love-filled beam

En-ters in, its light pro-claim-ing, Then with suns they seem a-flam-ing.

47. Helft mir Gott's Güte preisen
"These mercies we're adoring"

These mer-cies we're a-dor-ing, O Lord, who dwell'st a-bove,
Which Thou hast been re-stor-ing Through Christ, the Son of Love,

In Whom Thou wilt be pleased To grant this year en-su-ing Grace,

con-stant in well-do-ing, Till we're from sin re-leased.

48. Herr Gott, dich loben wir
"O help us, Lord, Thy servants crowned"

O help us, Lord, Thy ser-vants crowned, Who through Thy blood sal - va-tion found; May we in heav - en share Thy court And with Thy saints al - way re-sort. Thy peo-ple help, Lord Je - sus Christ; And all Thine her-i - tage as-sist; Nur-ture and watch them all, we pray, That they may dwell with Thee for aye.

49. Herr Jesu Christ, du höchstes Gut
"Lord Jesus Christ, my only Stay"

Lord Je - sus Christ, my on - ly Stay, To Thee will I be wend - ing:
My grief Thou know-est, canst al - lay; By Thee it shall be end - ing: It is ap-point-ed by Thy will; Thy plea-sure, Lord, may I ful-fil, Thine now and e'er re - main - ing.

50. Herr Jesu Christ, wahr'r Mensch und Gott
"O Lord, forgive our sins so great"

O Lord, for-give our sins so great; And help, that we in pa-tience wait Till our last hour on earth draws nigh, And that our faith with watch-ful eye May trust Thy Word e'er stead-fast-ly, Till bless-ed-ly we sleep in Thee.

51. Herr, wie du will't, so schick's mit mir
"Lord, as Thou wilt, deal Thou with me"

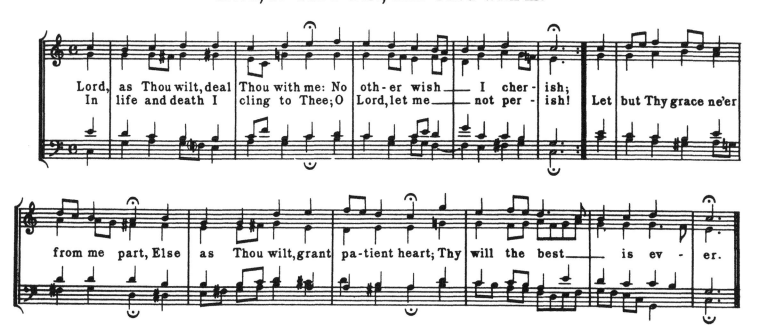

Lord, as Thou wilt, deal Thou with me: No oth-er wish I cher-ish;
In life and death I cling to Thee; O Lord, let me not per-ish!
Let but Thy grace ne'er from me part, Else as Thou wilt, grant pa-tient heart; Thy will the best is ev-er.

52. Ich freue mich in dir

"'Tis well! no more lament!"

'Tis well! no more la - ment! To Thee, O Je - sus, cling - ing,
Let earth, in frag-ments rent, To sud-den doom be spring - ing. O Je - sus, on - ly

Thine, For Thee a-lone I pine; On Thee, O Lord di - vine, I, dy - ing, now re - cline.

53. Jesu, der du meine Seele

"I believe, Lord; help my frailty"

I be-lieve, Lord; help my frail - ty: Let me nev - er be dis-mayed. Sin and death may

sore as-sail me; Thy strong arm is pres-ent aid. In Thy good-ness ev - er trust-ing,

Thee, Lord Je-sus, e'er be-hold-ing, Grant me ref-uge af - ter strife, Hap-py in e - ter-nal life.

54. Kommt her zu mir, spricht Gottes Sohn
"No child of man upon this earth"

No child of man up-on this earth For such a gift hath proved his worth: No ser-vice have we ren-dered. The love and grace which Christ sup-plies All earth-ly trea-sure far out-vies: A-tone-ment full He ten-dered.

55. Mit Fried' und Freud' ich fahr' dahin
"He is the Hope, the Saving Light"

He is the Hope, the Sav-ing Light, That hea-then na-tions need, And them who know Thee not a-right Will teach and lead; While all Is-rael's joy He is, His peo-ple's glo-ry, praise, and bliss.

56. Nun lasst uns Gott dem Herren
"His Word, Baptism, and Sacrament"

His Word, Bap-tism, and Sac-ra-ment Check ev-'ry sin-ful tor-ment; By

faith the sa-cred Spir-it Ap-plies His sav-ing mer-it.

57. Nun lob', mein' Seel', den Herren
"For, as a tender father"

For, as a ten-der fa-ther Hath pi-ty on his chil-dren here,
He in His arms will gath-er All who are His in child-like fear.

He knows how frail our pow-ers, Who but from dust are made: We

flour-ish as the flow-ers, And ev-en so——we fade. A

58. O Gott, du frommer Gott

"And grant me, Lord, to do"

59. O Herre Gott, dein göttlich Wort
"My trust is bold"

My trust is bold Thou'lt still up-hold, In dy-ing and in liv - - - ing,
Those who pur - sue As ser-vants true Thy Word, from heart be - liev - - - ing.

Great bliss ev'n now Thou dost be-stow On them: they ne'er shall per - ish. O

Lord, let me Be kept through Thee, In all my course me cher - - - ish.

60. O Welt, ich muss dich lassen
(Nun ruhen alle Wälder)
"Who could so rudely smite Thee"

Who could so rude-ly smite Thee, And mock at Thee, and spite Thee. Who wrong my Sav - ior

so? Thou art in-deed no sin - ner, As we and all our kin__ are; Nor of mis-do-ing canst Thou know.

61. Schwing' dich auf zu deinem Gott
"Lift thy head and proudly sing"

Lift thy head and proud-ly sing: Flee, de-spis-ed ser - pent! Why re-new'st thy dead-ly sting, Caus-ing fear and tor - ment? Christ in-deed hath bruised thy head, And me, through His sad - ness, From thee to Him - self hath led In the realms of glad - ness.

62. Straf mich nicht in deinem Zorn
"Let us watch then, pray with heed"

Let us watch then, pray with heed; God will prove our Hear - er;
For the hour of ut - most need Con-stant-ly draws near - er.
Saints will cheer, Sin-ners fear, When the trum-pet call - eth, Earth in ru - ins fall - eth.

63. Vater unser im Himmelreich

"Thy will be done on earth, O Lord"

Thy will be done on earth, O Lord, As where in heav'n Thou art a - dored! Pa-
tience in time of grief be-stow, O - be - dience true through weal and woe, Strength
tempt - ing wish - es to con - trol That thwart Thy will with - in the soul.

64. Von Gott will ich nicht lassen

"This is the Father's pleasure"

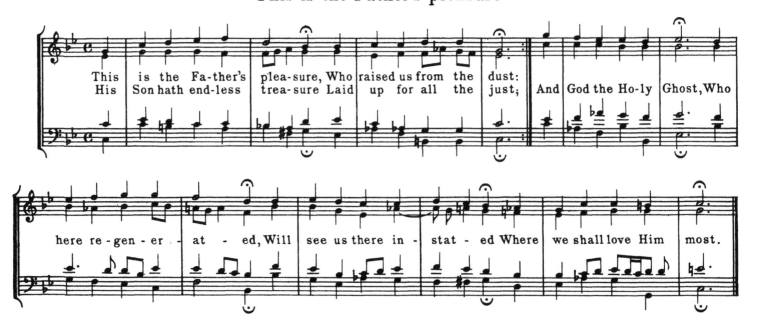

This is the Fa-ther's plea-sure, Who raised us from the dust:
His Son hath end-less trea-sure Laid up for all the just; And God the Ho-ly Ghost, Who
here re-gen-er - at - ed, Will see us there in - stat - ed Where we shall love Him most.

65. Wachet auf, ruft uns die Stimme

"Glory unto Thee be given"

66. Warum betrübst du dich, mein Herz
"What here may shine"

What here may shine I all re-sign If the e-ter-nal crown be mine That through Thy bit-ter death Thou gain-edst, O Lord Christ, for me: For this, for this, I cry to Thee!

67. Was mein Gott will, das g'scheh' allzeit
"What my God wills is best alway"

What my God wills is best al-way, And ev-er best His plea - - sure;
His help He nev-er will de-lay To those who trust full mea - - sure.

To those in need God will give heed, And chast-en gen-tly ev - - er; To

those who trust He will be just, And will for-sake them nev - - er.

68. Wir Christenleut'
"Sin brought us grief"

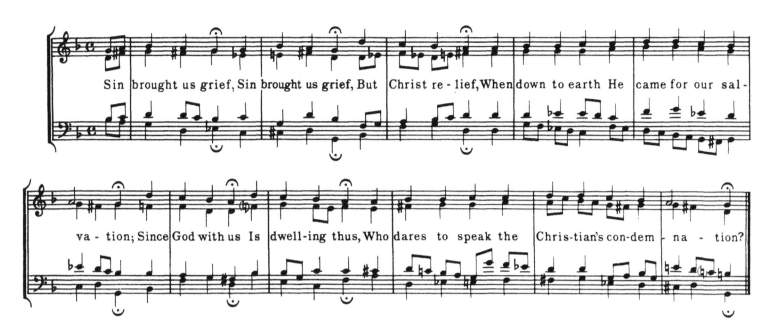

Sin brought us grief, Sin brought us grief, But Christ re - lief, When down to earth He came for our sal-va - tion; Since God with us Is dwell-ing thus, Who dares to speak the Chris-tian's con-dem - na - tion?

69. Allein zu dir, Herr Jesu Christ
"Glory to God in highest heaven"

Glo - ry to God in high - est heav'n, The Fa - ther of e - ter - nal___ love;
To His dear Son, for sin - ners giv'n, Whose watch-ful grace we_____ dai-ly prove;

To God the Ho - ly Ghost on high: Oh, ev - er be His com-fort nigh, And teach us, free from

sin and fear, To please___ Him here, And serve Him in the sin - - less sphere!

70. Christ, unser Herr, zum Jordan kam
"So that we, all with one accord"

So that we, all with one ac-cord, To heav-en's por-tal press - ing, May then in Thy do -main, O Lord, E - ter -nal hymns be stress - ing: To hail Thee King and love Thee most, Far o - ver ev -'ry ri - val, God, Fa - ther, Son, and Ho - ly Ghost, The source of life e - ter - nal, Three Per-sons in one be - ing.

71. Christum wir sollen loben schon
"Honor to Thee, O Christ, be paid"

Hon - or to Thee, O Christ, be paid, Pure off - spring of a ho - ly

72. Freu' dich sehr, o meine Seele

"For the Baptist's voice is crying"

73. Freuet euch, ihr Christen

"Jesu, guard and guide Thy members"

Je-su, guard and guide Thy mem-bers; Fill Thy breth-ren with Thy grace; Hear their pray'rs in

ev-'ry place; Quick-en now life's faint-est em-bers; Grant all Chris-tians, far and near,

Ho-ly peace, a glad New Year. Joy, O joy, be-yond all glad-ness! Christ hath done a-

way with sad-ness. Hence, all sor-row, all re-pin-ing! For the Sun of grace is shin-ing.

74. Herzlich lieb hab' ich dich, o Herr

"O Lord, I love Thee from my heart"

O Lord, I love Thee from my heart; I pray Thee nev-er more de-part With

I scorn the rich-est earth-ly lot; E'en heav'n it-self at-tracts me not If

help and grace to cheer me; Through all my heart's se-ver-est pains, In Thee my con-fi-

I can feel Thee near me.

dence re-mains; That Sav-ior shall my com-fort be Who by His blood hath pur-chased me. O

Je-sus Christ, O Je-sus Christ, my God and Lord, Be near, ac-cord-ing to Thy Word.

75. Ich dank' dir, lieber Herre
"True faith to me vouchsafe, Lord"

True faith to me vouch-safe, Lord, Through Je-sus Christ, Thy Son; And all my sins so

way - ward Hence-forth help me to shun. For Thou wilt ne'er re-fuse me, Thy prom-ise hold-eth

fast, From sin-ful bur-den free me, And bring me home at last.

bring me home

bring me home

76. Ist Gott mein Schild und Helfersmann
"With God my guard and shepherd true"

With | God my guard and | shep-herd true, Mis- | for-tune can-not | me sub-due: From

foes He will de- | liv- er. The | grief and pain they | plan for me Up- | on them-selves shall

turn-ed__ be, For | God my Friend is | ev- er, For | God my Friend is | ev- er.

77. Jesu, meine Freude
"Jesus, priceless Treasure"

Je-sus, price-less | Trea- sure, | Source of pur-est | plea- sure, | Tru-est Friend to | me!
O how long I've | pant- ed, | And my heart hath | faint- ed, | Thirst-ing, Lord, for | Thee!

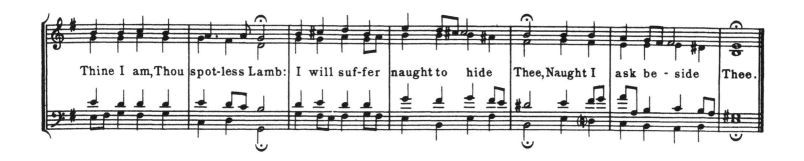

78. Jesu, meine Freude

"In Thine arms I rest me"

79. Jesu, meine Freude
"Hence with earthly treasure!"

80. Jesu, meine Freude

"Fare thee well that errest"

81. Jesu, meine Freude
"Hence, all fears and sadness!"

Hence, all fears and sad - ness! For the Lord of glad - ness, Je - sus, en - ters in.
They who love the Fa - ther, Though the storms may gath - er, Still have peace with - in.

Yea, what-e'er I here must bear, Still in Thee lies pur-est plea - sure, Je-su, price-less Trea - sure.

82. Komm, Jesu, komm
"I give myself into Thy pleasure"

I give my - self in - to Thy plea - sure And bid a - dieu: world,

now good night! Then, when my life - span fills its mea - sure, From earth my soul will

take its flight, To dwell with Je - sus, there to hov - er; For Je - sus is and

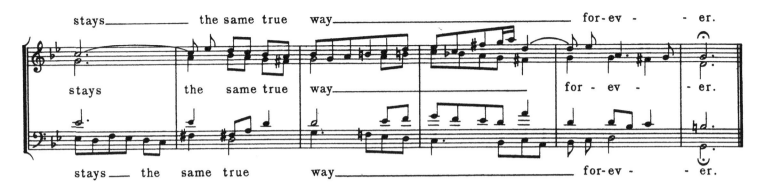

stays_____ the same true way_____ for-ev - - er.

stays the same true way_____ for - ev - - er.

stays__ the same true way_____ for-ev - - er.

83. Liebster Gott, wann werd' ich sterben?
"Ruler over dead and living"

84. Nun bitten wir den heiligen Geist
"Thou sweetest Love! pray we heartily"

Thou sweet-est Love! pray____ we heart-i - ly, Let us feel love-

sparks a - maz-ing-ly, Let us from our heart____ be t'each oth - er ten - -der
oth - er
oth - er

mer - -cy,
And to the broth-er-ly mind sur - ren - -der: Have____ mer - -cy,____ Lord!
And to
And to

85. Nun freut euch, lieben Christen g'mein
"I stand beside Thy manger here"

I stand be-side Thy man-ger here, O Je - su, life im - plant-ing; Take
I come to bring with joy sin-cere The things Thou hast been grant-ing.   Thou—it is my

soul and thought, Heart, mind, and faith, to Thee now brought: I pray that they may please Thee.

86. Schmücke dich, o liebe Seele
"Jesus, Bread of life from heaven"

Je - sus, Bread of life from heav - - en, Nev - er be Thou vain - ly giv - - en,
Nor I to my hurt in - vit - ed; Be my love with love re - quit - - ed;

Let me learn its depths__ in - deed While on Thee my soul__ doth__ feed;

Let me, here so rich - ly blest, Be here - af - ter, too,__ Thy__ guest.

87. Singen wir aus Herzensgrund
"God, Who ordained the earth so fair"

earth so_____
sup - pli -

Planned for_____
That our_____

e - qual
may grow

God, Who or - dained the earth__ so fair, Planned for food with e - qual care:
We thank our Lord and sup - pli - cate That__ our spir - it may__ grow great,

sent the
we may

beasts their
love Him

Hill and vale__ He sent__ the rain, That all beasts their food__ might gain; From the
That in all__ things we__ may know How to love Him, how__ to grow; Let us

earth's store, wine and bread God sup-ply-ing, kept us fed, To a life of plen-ty led.
praise His name so grand, In Christ's name tak-ing our stand, "Gra-ti-as" from all de-mand.

88. Verleih' uns Frieden gnädiglich
"Grant us Thy peace, we pray Thee, Lord"

peace, we pray Thee, Lord, To com-fort us while liv - ing.

peace, we pray Thee, Lord, To com-fort us while liv-ing. There

Grant us Thy peace, we pray Thee, Lord, To com-fort us while liv - - ing. There

is none oth - er with the sword Can work our sins' for-giv - - ing But Thou, dear Lord e'er-

last - ing. Grant to the heads and all our mag-is - trates Peace and good re - gen - cy, That

un - der their e - dicts We may all have a qui - et and a peace-ful life - span,

Liv-ing in all pi - e - ty And de-cen-cy. A - - - men.

89. Wär' Gott nicht mit uns diese Zeit
"Thanks be to God, Who from the pit"

Thanks be to God, Who from the pit Snatched us when it was gap - ing, Our
was___ gap - ing,

souls, like birds that break the net, To the blue skies es - cap - ing: The snare is bro - ken—
es - - cap - ing:

earth___ and heav - en.
we are free! The Lord, our Help - er, prais - ed be, The God of earth and heav - en.
earth___ and heav - en.
earth___ and heav - en.

90. Welt, ade! ich bin dein müde
"World, farewell! Of thee I'm tired"

SOPRANO I
SOPRANO II
World, fare - well! Of thee I'm tired;___ Now t'ward heav'n my
ALTO
World, fare - well!___ Of thee I'm tired; Now t'ward heav'n my
TENOR
BASS

91. Werde munter, mein Gemüthe
"Though I lapsed, and straying wander"

*These small notes are to be used instead of the preceding notes when the repeat is made.